RAC

Road Atlas Great Bri
& Ireland 1998

contents

City and Town Centre Plans ii
Ireland vi

Main map section 8
scale 1:250,000 (approx. 4 miles to 1 inch)

Index to place names 84

SYMBOLS USED IN MAIN MAP SECTION

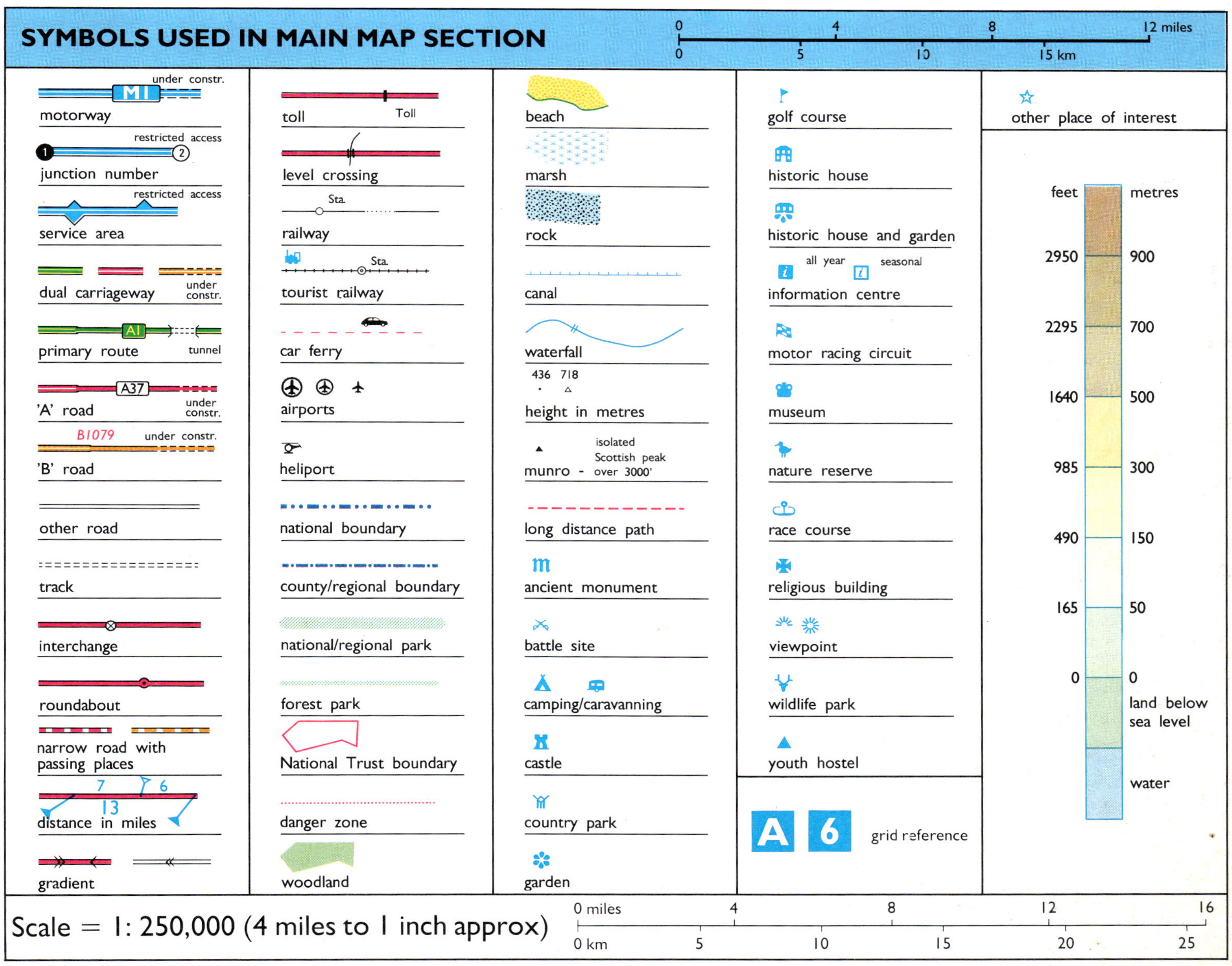

W1

RAC Road Atlas Great Britain & Ireland 1998

Published by West One (Trade) Publishing Ltd.,
Portland House, 4 Great Portland Street,
London W1N 5AA

New 1998 Edition

Printed in Great Britain

ABERDEEN

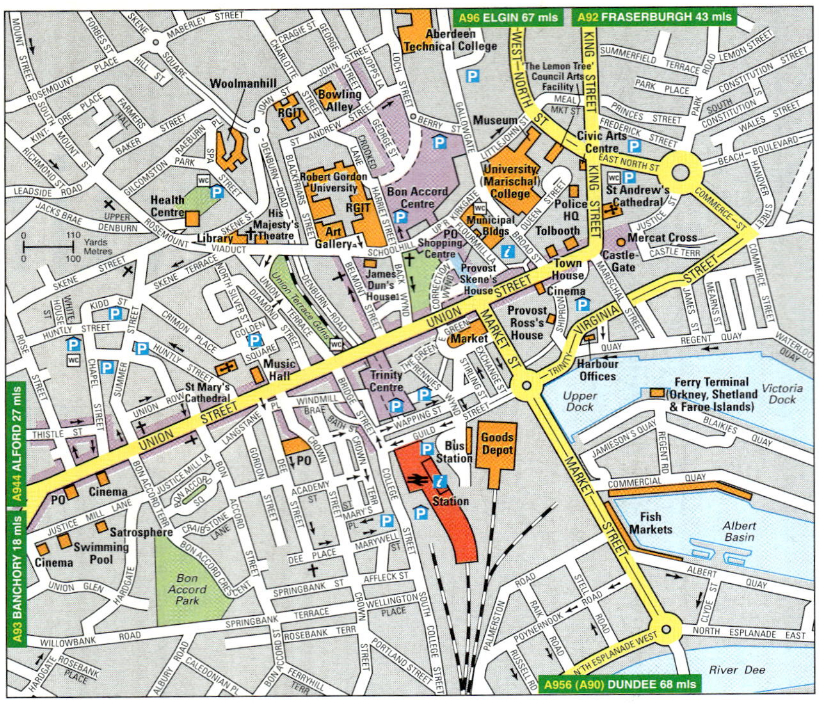

BRISTOL

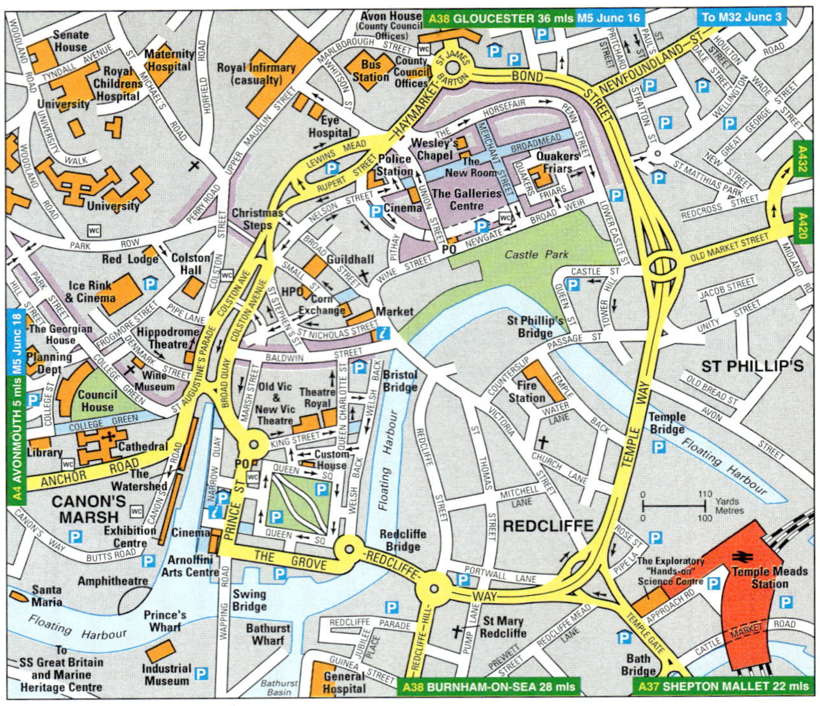

BATH

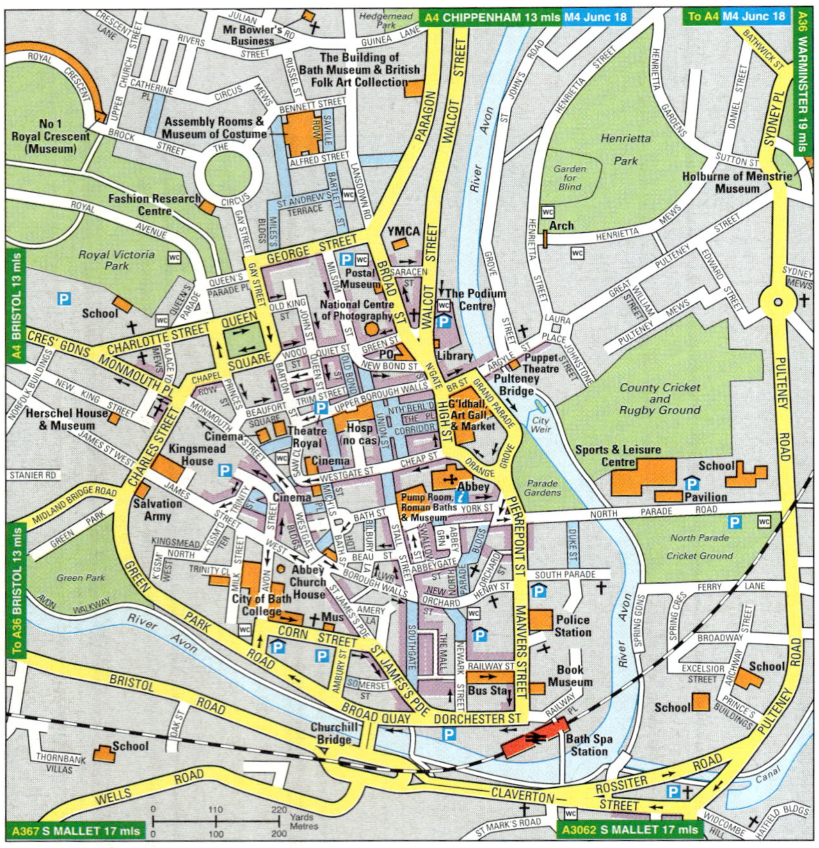

CAMBRIDGE

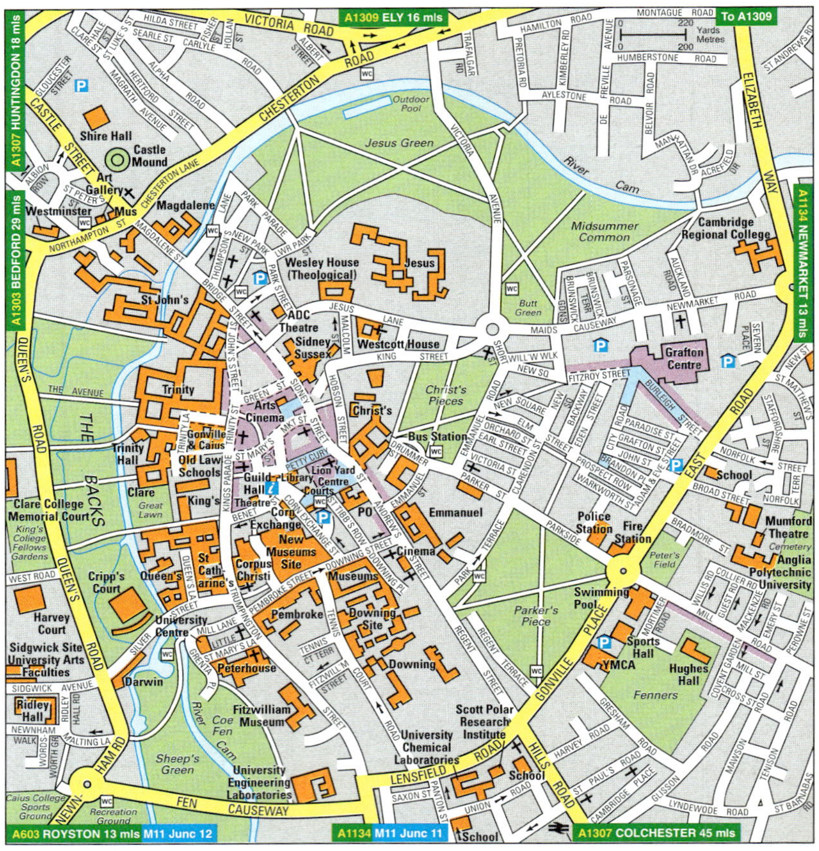

BIRMINGHAM

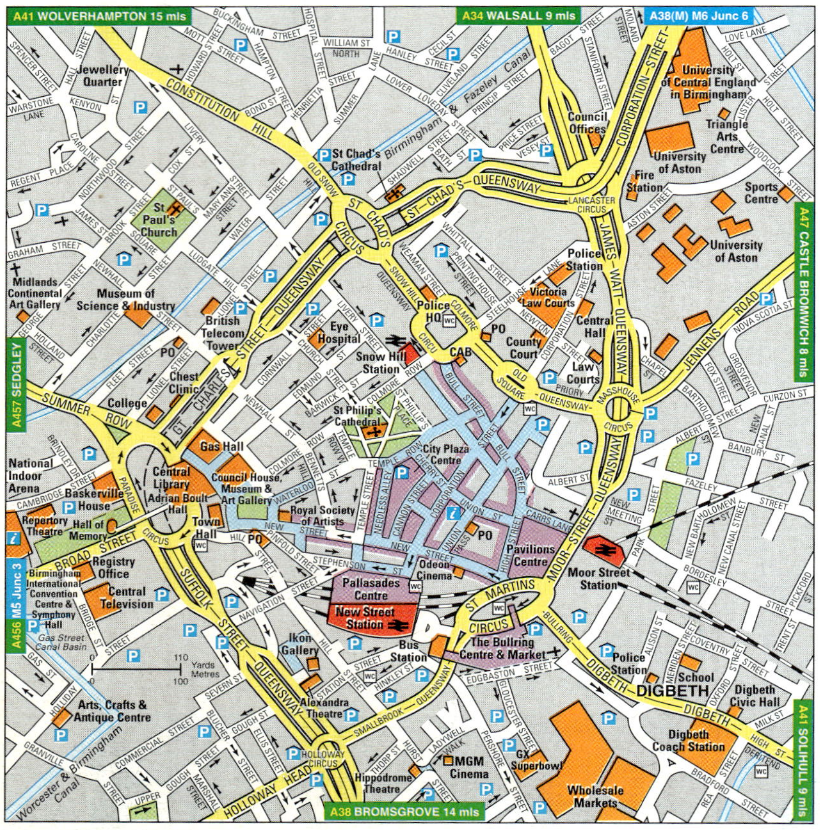

CARDIFF

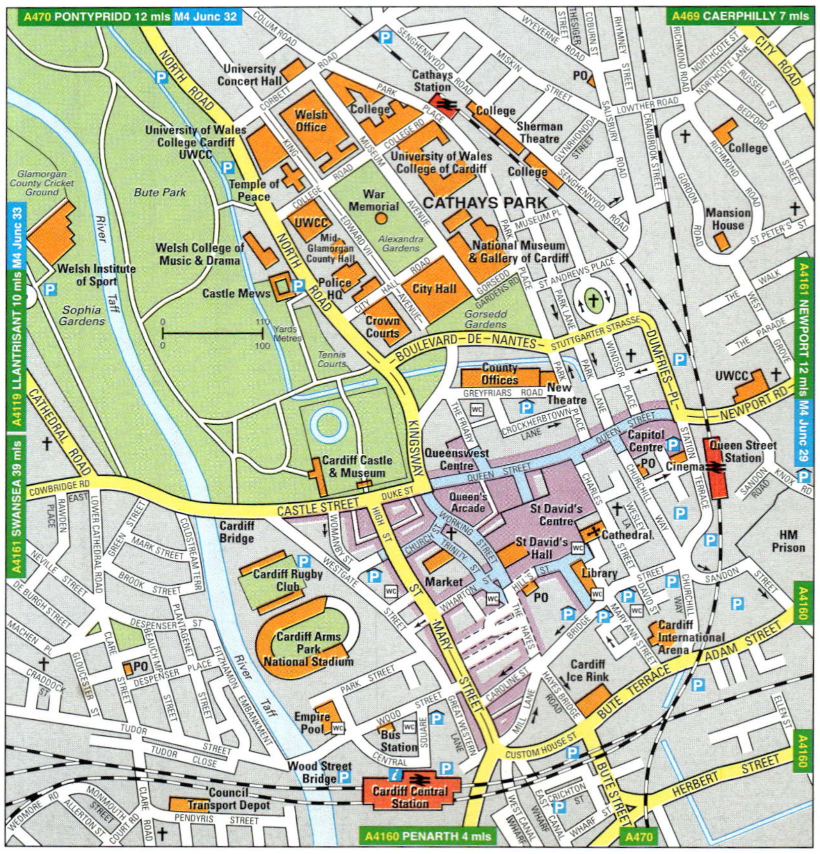

COVENTRY

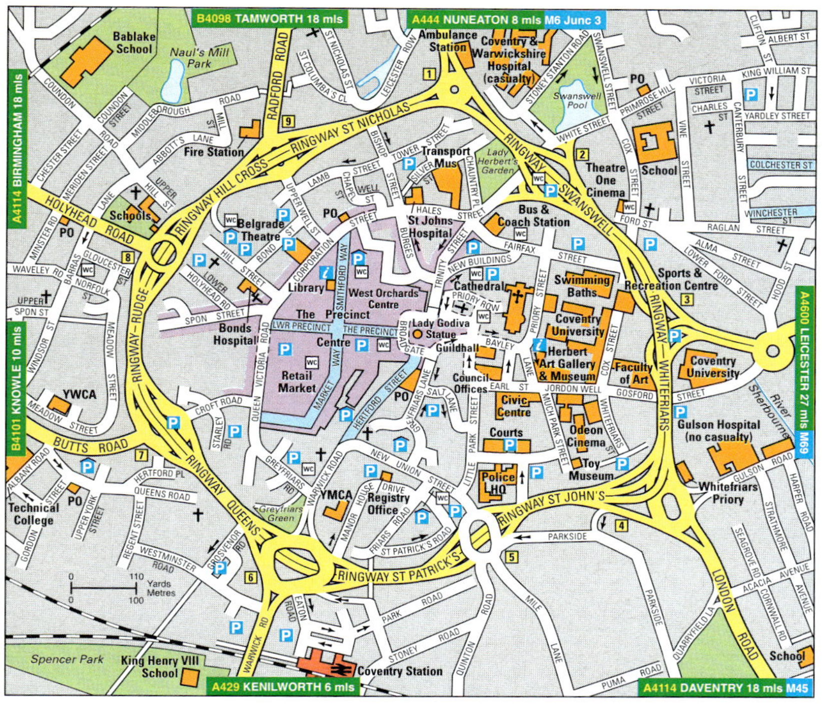

HULL

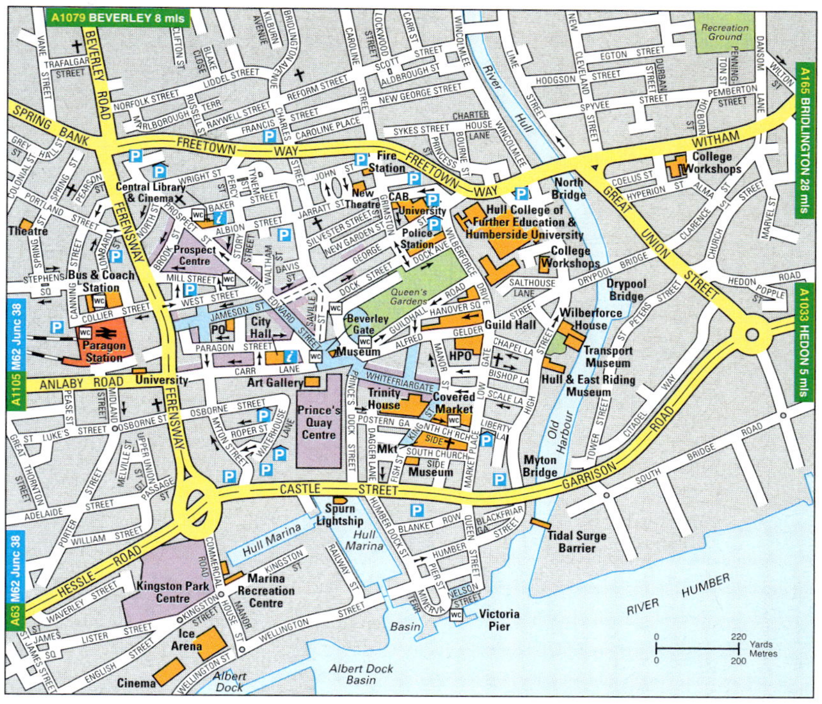

EDINBURGH

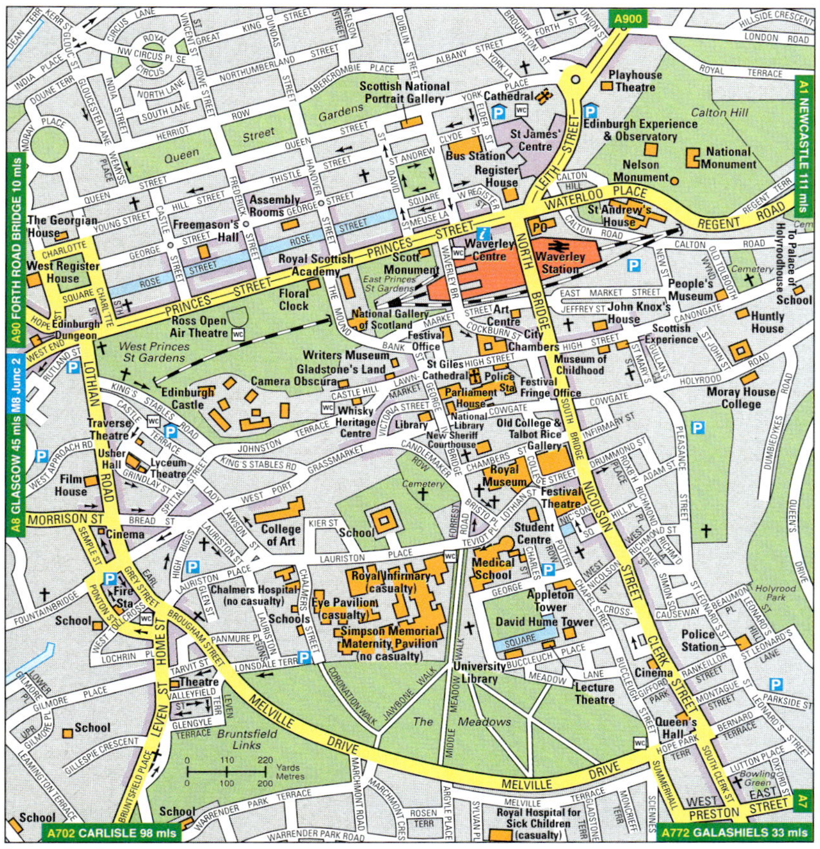

LEEDS

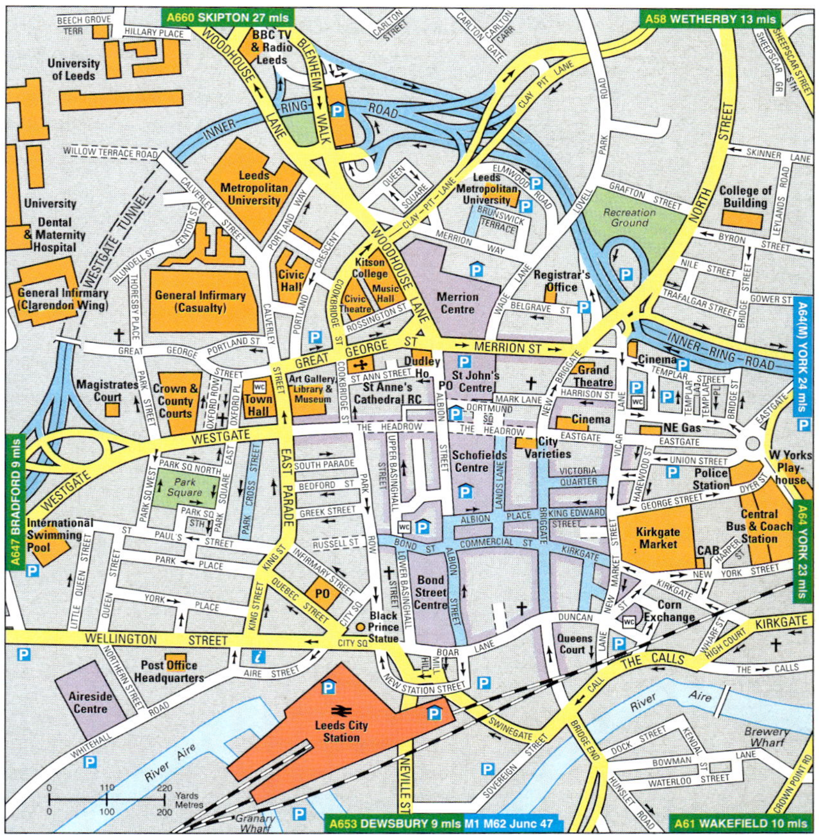

GLASGOW

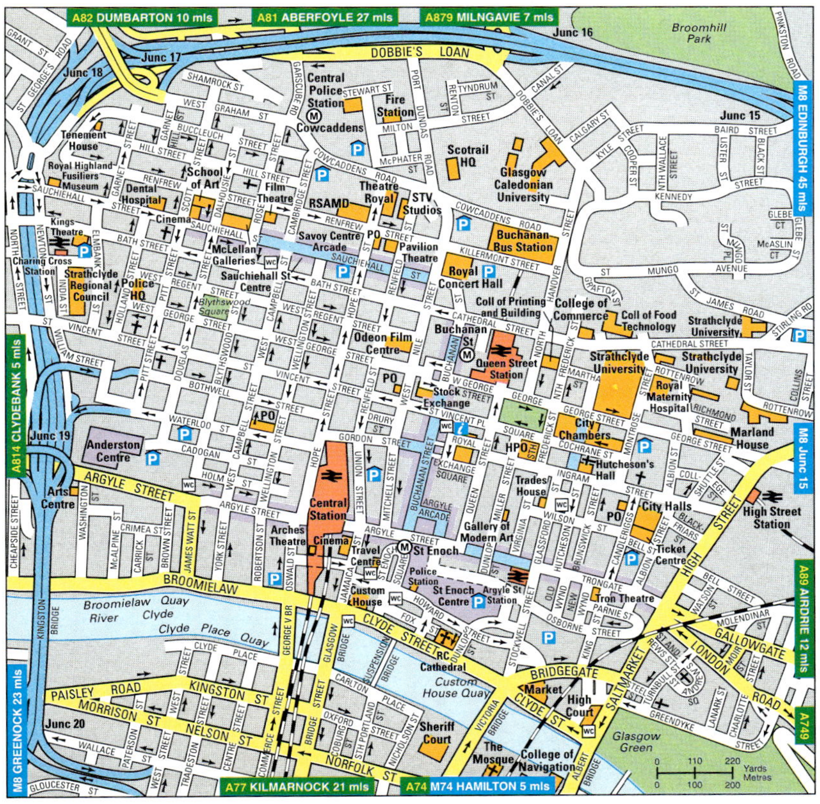

LEICESTER

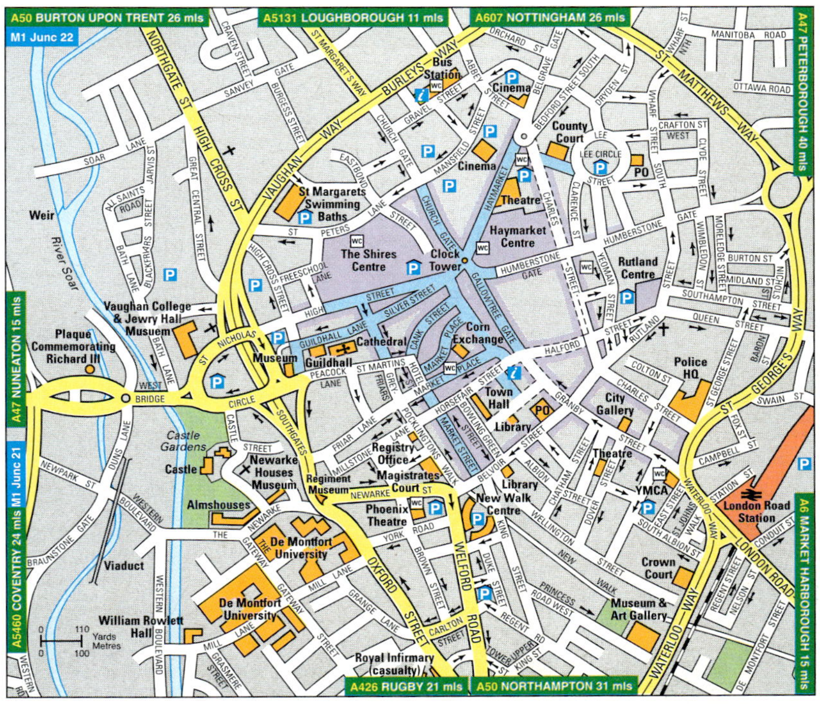

LIVERPOOL

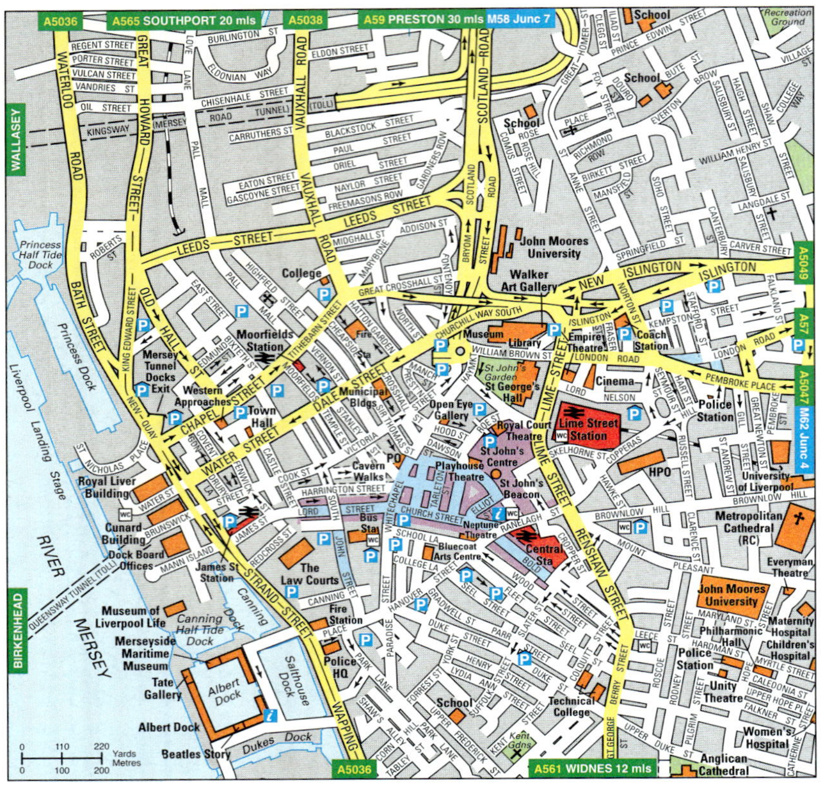

NEWCASTLE UPON TYNE

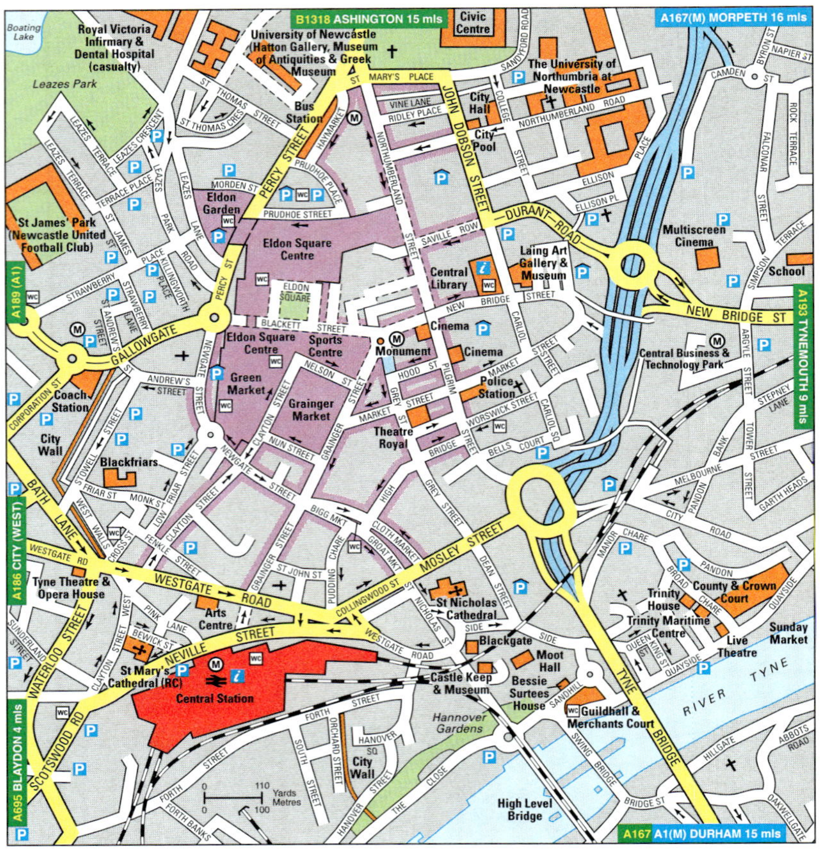

MANCHESTER

NORWICH

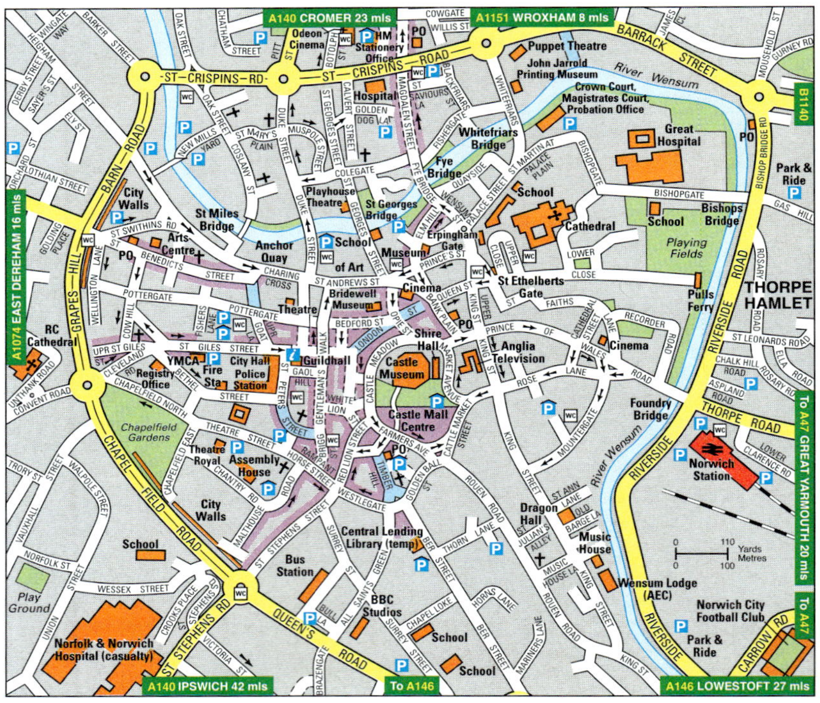

MILTON KEYNES

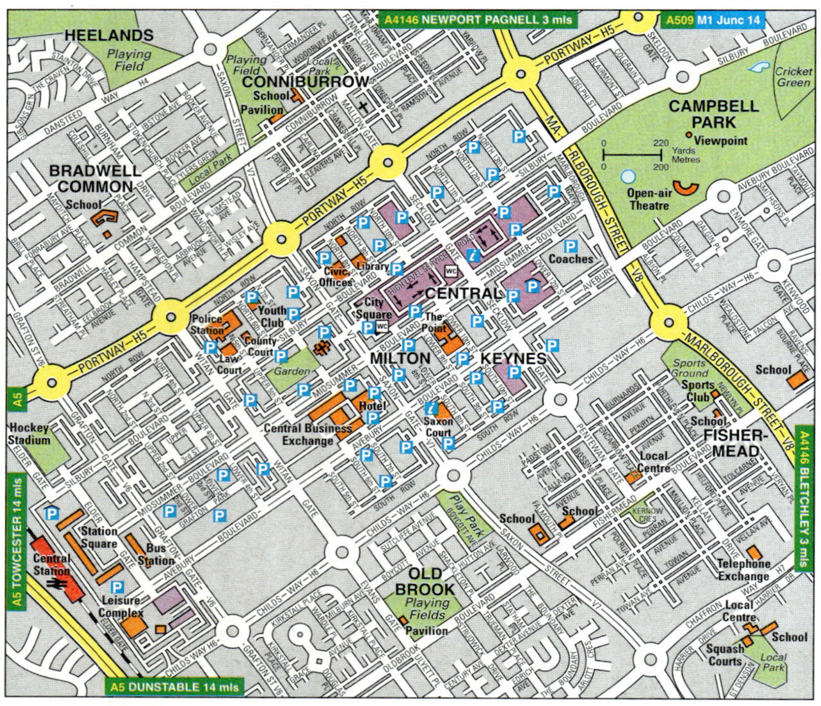

NOTTINGHAM

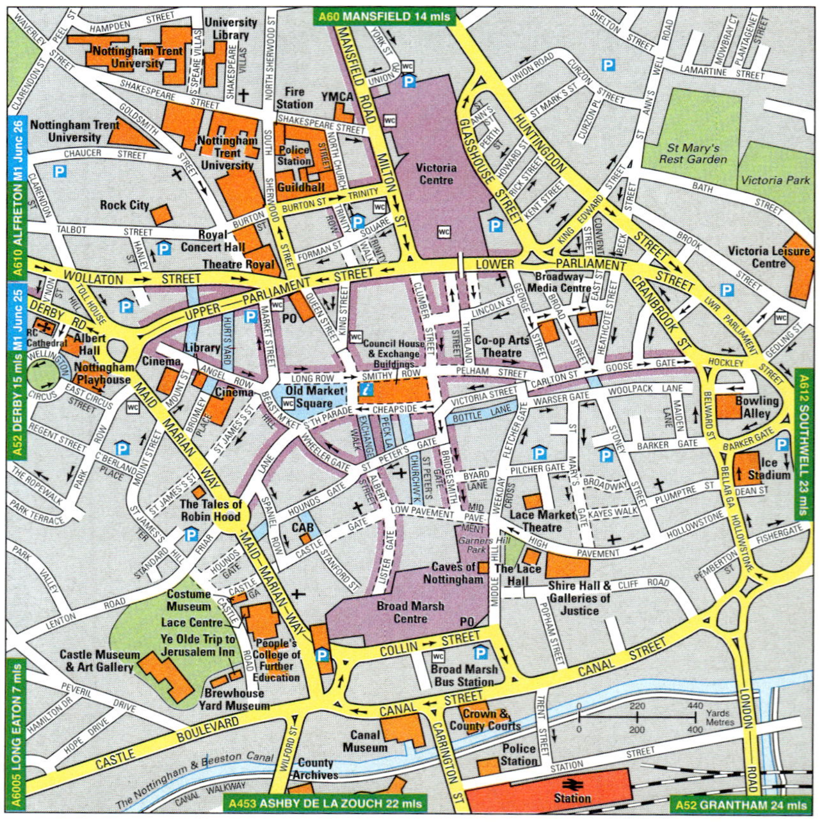

OXFORD

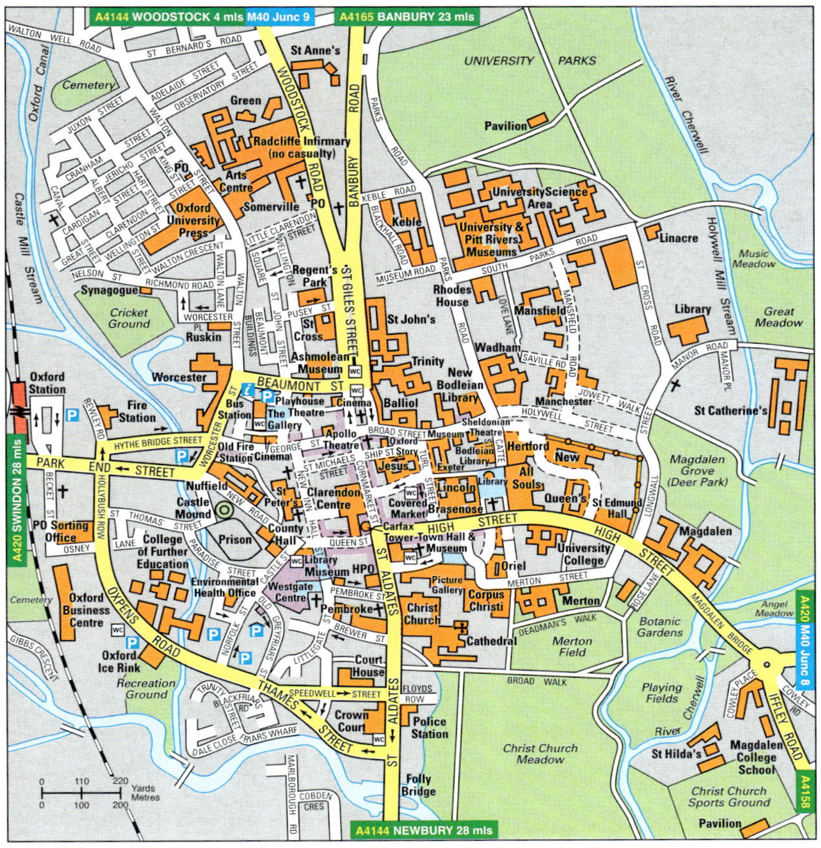

STRATFORD-UPON-AVON

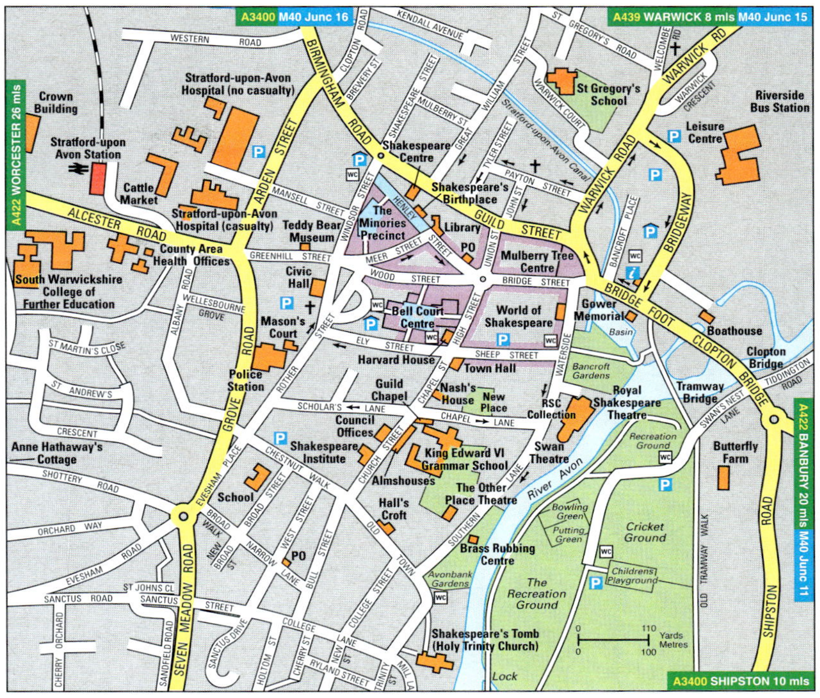

PORTSMOUTH

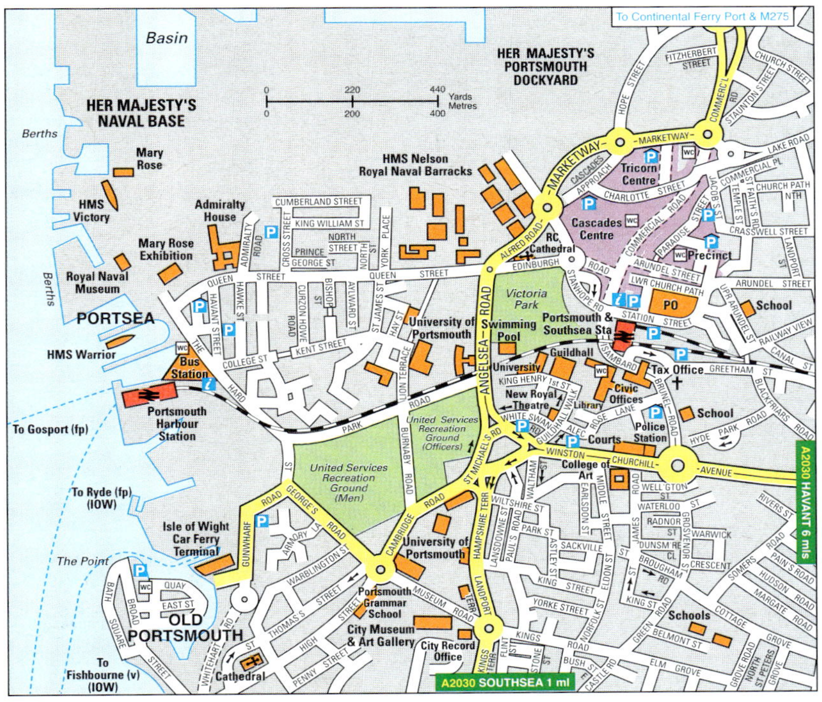

WOLVERHAMPTON

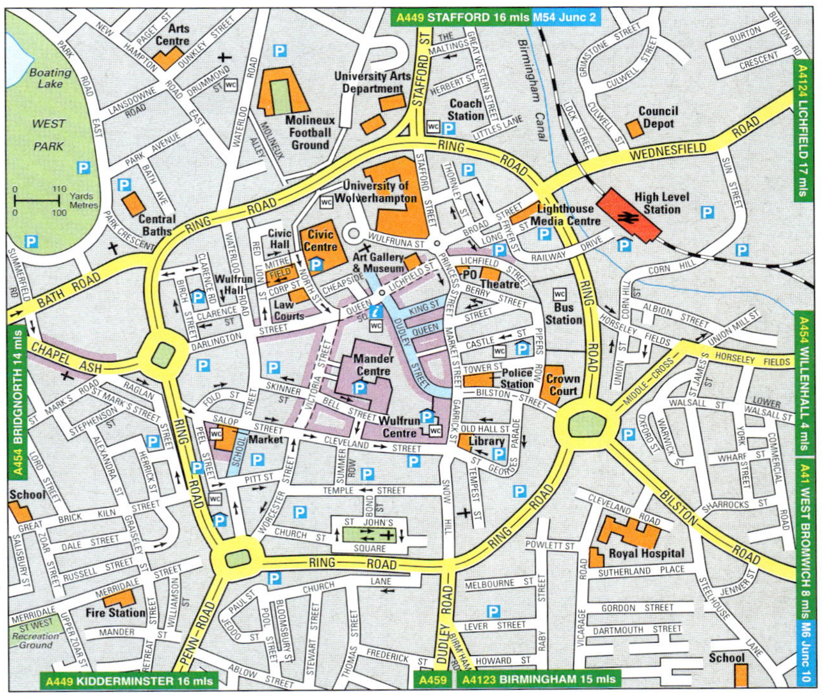

SHEFFIELD

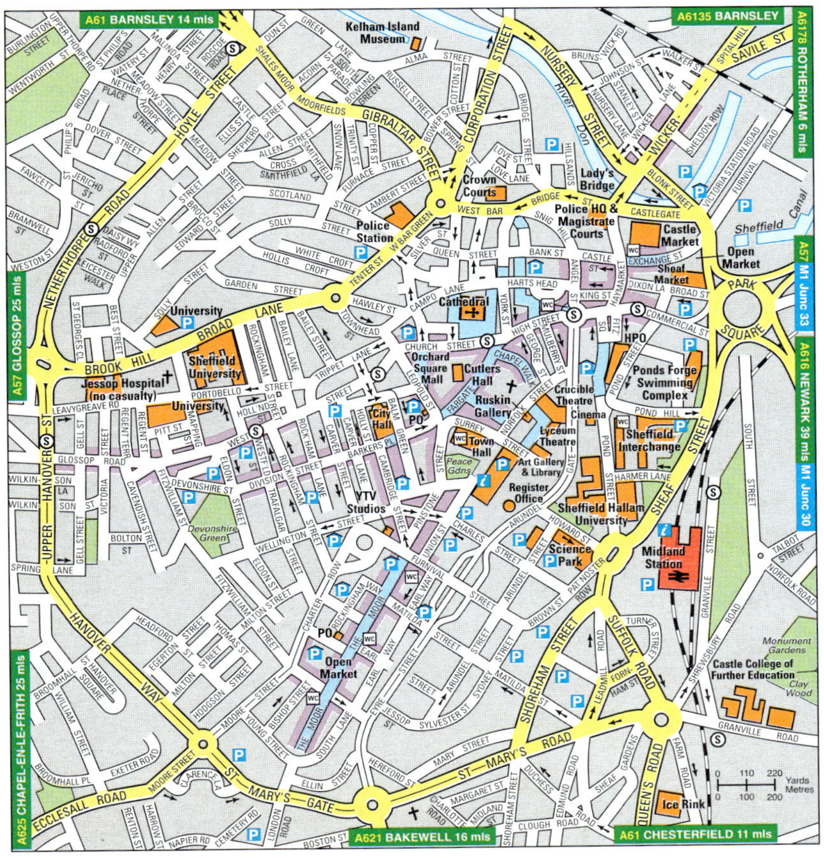

YORK

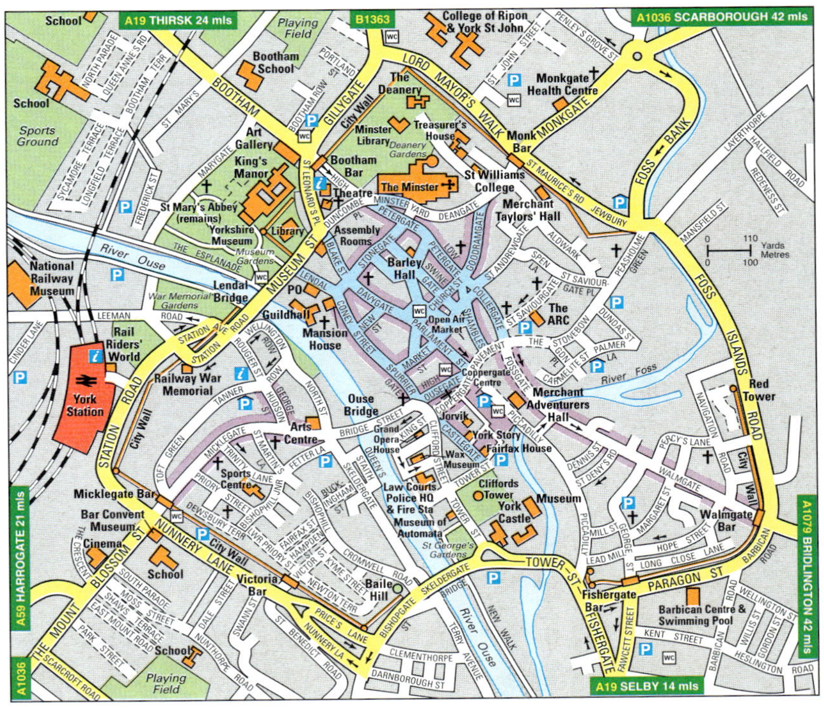

BELFAST

Academy St. B2
Adelaide St. B4
Albert Bridge D4
Albert St. A3
Albion St. A5
Alfred St. B4
Amelia St. A4
Ann St. B3/C3
Antrim Rd. A1
Apsley St. B4
Arthur St. B3
Athol St. A4
Ballarat St. D4
Bank St. B3
Bankmore St. B4
Bedford St. B4
Berry St. B3
Blythe St. A5
Bond St. C4
Botanic Ave. A5
Boyd St. A2
Bradbury Pl. A5
Bridge End D3
Bridge St. B3
Brown St. A2
Brown's Sq. A2
Bruce St. A4
Brunswick St. B4
Callender St. B3
Cameron St. B5
Carlisle Parade A1
Carlisle Rd. A1
Carlisle Ter. A1
Carrick Hill A3
Castle Lane B3
Castle Pl. B3
Castle St. A3
Chapel Lane B3
Charles Street Sth. A5
Charlotte St. B5
Chichester St. B3
Church Lane C3
Clarence St. B4
Clifton St. A1
College Court A3
College Sq. East A3
College Sq. North A3
College St. A3
Cooke Court C5
Cooke Mews C5
Cooke St. C5
Copeland St. B5
Cornmarket B3
Corporation Sq. C1
Corporation St. C2
Cromac St. C4
Cromwell Rd. B5
Custom House Sq. C2
Dalton St. D2
Denmark St. A1
Divis St. A3
Donegall Pass B5
Donegall Pl. B3
Donegall Quay C2
Donegall Rd. A5
Donegall Sq. East B3
Donegall Sq. North B3
Donegall Sq. South B4
Donegall Sq. West B3
Donegall St. B2
Dublin Rd. B5
Dunbar Link C2
Dunbar St. B2
Durham St. A3
Earl St. C1
East Bridge St. C4
Edward St. B2
Eglinton St. A1
Eliza St. C4
Elm St. B5
Fleetwood St. A1
Fountain St. B3
Fox Row A3
Francis St. A3
Franklin St. B4
Frederick St. B1
Friendly St. C4
Gaffikin St. A5
Galway St. A3
Gamble St. C2
Gardiner St. A2
Glenalpin St. A5
Glengall St. A4
Gloucester St. C3
Gordon St. B2
Grace St. C4
Great George's St. B1/C1
Great Victoria St. A4
Gresham St. B2
Grosvenor Rd. A4
Hamill St. A3
Hamilton St. C4
Hardcastle St. B5
Hart St. B5
Hector St. B2
Henry Pl. A1
Henry St. B1
High St. B3
Hill St. B2
Hope St. A4
Howard St. A4
Institution Pl. A3
John St. A3
Joy St. B4
Kent St. A2
King Street Mews A3
King St. A3
Laganbank Rd. C3
Laganview St. D3
Lancaster St. B1
Library St. A2
Lime Court A2
Lincoln Ave. A1
Lindsay St. B5
Linen Hall St. B4
Linfield Rd. A4
Little Donegall St. B2
Little May St. B4
Little Patrick St. B1
Little Victoria St. B4
Little York St. B1
Lower Stanfield St. C4
Macart Rd. D2
Majestic Drive A5
Marquis St. A3
Maryville St. B5
May St. B4
McAuley St. C4
McClintock St. B4
McClure St. B5
Middlepath St. D3
Millfield A2
Montgomery St. B3
Murray St. A3
Musgrave St. C3
Napier St. A5
Nelson St. B2/C1
North Queen St. B1
North St. A2/B2
Norwood St. A4
Oak Way B5
Ormeau Ave. B4
Ormeau Embankment D5
Ormeau Rd. C5
Ormeau St. C5
Oxford St. C3
Pakenham St. B5
Park Parade D5
Peter's Hill A2
Pilot St. C1
Pim St. A1
Pine Way B5
Postnett St. B5
Prince's Dock St. C1
Prince's St. C3
Queen Elizabeth Br. C3
Queen St. A3
Queen's Bridge C3
Queen's Quay Rd. D2
Queen's Quay D2
Queen's Rd. D2
Queen's Sq. C2
Raphael St. C4
Regent St. A1
River Ter. C5
Rosemary St. B3
Rotterdam St. D3
Rowland Way A4
Royal Ave. B2/3
Russell St. B4
Salisbury St. B5
Samuel St. A2
Sandy Row A4/5
Scott St. A5
Scrabo St. D2
Short Strand D3
Short St. C1
Skipper St. B2
Smithfield Sq. A2
Stanhope Drive A2
Stanley St. A3
Station Street Flyover D3
Station St. D2
Steam Mill Lane C2
Stephen St. A2
Stewart St. C4
Stroud St. A5
Sydenham Rd. D2
Talbot St. B2
Thomas St. B1
Tomb St. C2
Townsend St. A2
Union St. A2
Upper Arthur St. B3
Upper Garfield St. B2
Upper Library St. A2
Ventry St. A4
Vernon St. B5
Victoria Parade B1
Victoria Sq. C3
Victoria St. C3
Walnut St. B5
Waring St. B2
Wellington Pl. A3
Wellington St. A3
Wellwood St. A4
Welsh St. C4
Westlink A2
Wilson St. A2
Wine Tavern St. A2
York Lane B1
York St. B1

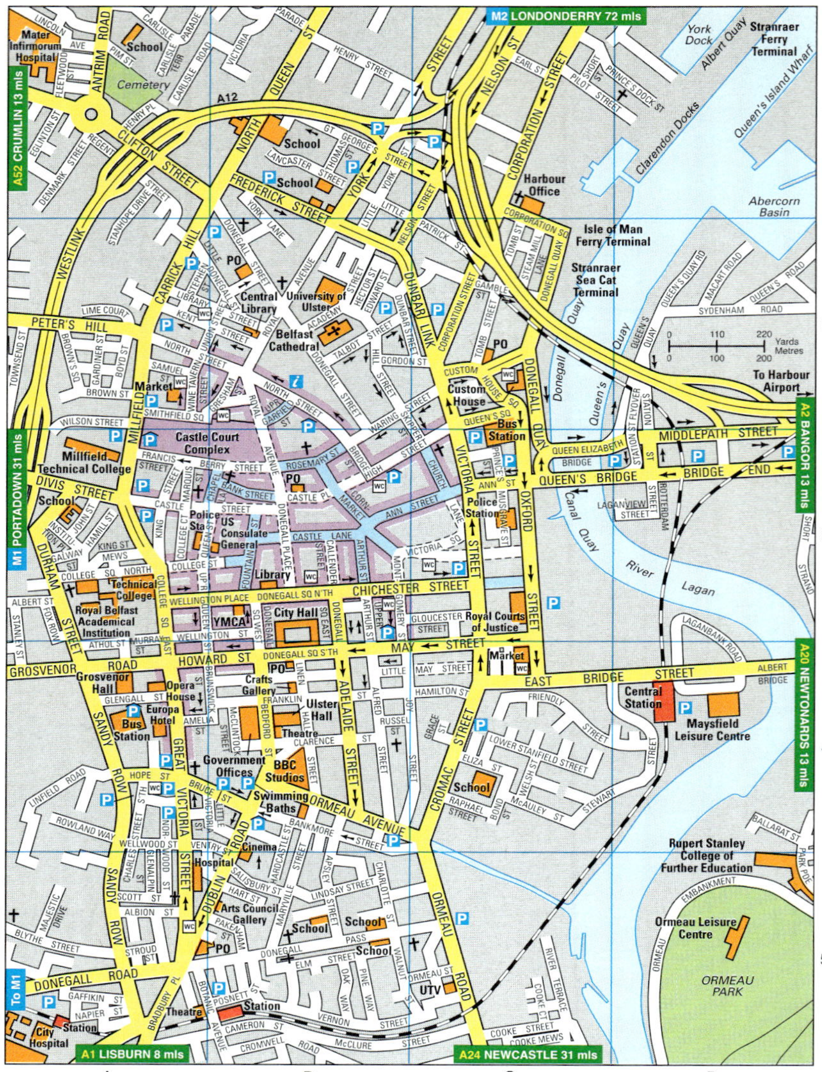

DUBLIN

Abbey St. C2
Adelaide Rd. C4
Amiens St. D2
Arran Quay B2
Aston Quay C2
Aughrim St. B2
Aungier St. C3
Baggot St. Lower D4
Ballybough Rd. D1
Batchelor's Walk C2
Benbulin Rd. A4
Berkeley Rd. C1
Blackhorse Ave. A1
Brackenhall Pl. B2
Cabra Rd. B1
Camden St. C4
Capel St. C2
Chesterfield Ave. A2
Church St. C2
City Quay D2
Clanbrassil St. Lower B4
Connaught Rd. B1
Conyngham Rd. A2
Cork St. B3
Crumlin Rd. A4
Custom House Quay D2
Dame St. C3
Davitt Rd. A4
Dawson St. C3
Dolphin Rd. A4
Dolphin's Barn B4
Eastwall Rd. D1
Eden Quay C2
Ellis Quay B2
Fenian St. D3
Gardiner St. Upper C1
Gardiner St. Lower C2
Georges Quay D2
Grafton St. C3
Grand Parade C4
Grand Canal St. D3
Grand Canal Quay D3
Grangegorman Upper B1
Haddlington Rd. D4
Hannover St. D3
Harcourt St. C4
Henry St. C2
High St. C3
Infirmary Rd. A2
Innis Quay B3/C3
James St. B3
Kildare St. C3
King St. North B2
Leeon St. Lower C4/D4
Leeson St Upper D4
Macken St. D3
Manor St. B2
Marowbone La. B3
Mary St. C2
Merrion Sq. D3
Mespil Rd. D4
Mount St. Lower D3
Mourne Rd. A4
Nassau St. C3
Navan Rd. A1
New St. South C3/C4
North Circular Rd. B1/C1
North Wall Quay D2
North Strand Rd. D1
O'Connell St. C2
Old Cabra Rd. A1
Old Kilmainham A3
Parnell Rd. B4
Parnell St. C2
Patrick St. C3
Pearse St. D3
Pembroke St. D4
Pembrole Rd. D4
Phibsborough Rd. B1
Portland Row D1
Prussia St. B1/B2
Ratoath Rd. A1
Sean McDermott St. C2/D2
Sheriff St. Lower D2
Sir John Rogerson's Quay D2
South Circular Rd. A3/A4/B4
St John's Rd. West A3
St James Walk A4
Summerhill C1/D1
The Coombe B3
Thomas St. West B3
Townsend St. C2/D3
Upper Dorset St. C1
Usher's Quay B3
Victoria Quay B3
Waterloo Rd. D4
Wellington Quay C3
Western Square C2
Wolfe Tone Quay B2
York St. C3

INDEX TO IRELAND

Aasleagh B4
Abbeyfeale B6
Abbeyleix D5
Anascaul A6
Antrim E3
Ardara C2
Ardee E4
Ardglass F3
Arklow E6
Armagh E3
Ashbourne E5
Ashford E5
Askeaton B6
Athboy E4
Athenry C5
Athleague C4
Athlone D5
Athy E5
Aughnacloy E3
Bailieborough E4
Balbriggan E4
Balla B4
Ballaghaderreen C4
Ballina B3
Ballinagh D4
Ballinamore D4
Ballinasloe C5
Ballinrobe B4
Ballybay E4
Ballybrack E5
Ballycastle E2
Ballyclare F3
Ballycroy B3
Ballydehob B8
Ballyhaunis C4
Ballyhillin D1
Ballyjamesduff D4
Ballyliffen D2
Ballylongford B6
Ballymahon D4
Ballymakeery B7
Ballymena E2
Ballymoe C4
Ballymoney E2
Ballynahinch F3
Ballyragget D6
Ballyshannon C3
Ballysodare C3
Ballyvaughan B5
Baltinglass E5
Banbridge E3
Bandon C7
Bangor F3
Bangor Erris B3
Bantry B7
BELFAST F3
Belleek D3
Belleek E3
Belmullet B3
Belturbet D4
Bessbrook E3
Birdhill C6
Birr D5
Borris-in-Ossory D5
Borrisokane C5
Borrisoleigh C6
Boyle C4
Bray E5
Bridge End D2
Brittas E5
Bunbeg C2
Buncanra D2
Bunclody E6
Bundoran C3
Butler's Bridge D4
Buttevant C7
Cahir C6
Cahirciveen A7
Callan D6
Carlow E6
Carndonagh D2
Carnlough F2
Carrick-on-Shannon D4
Carrick C3
Carrick-on-Suir D6
Carrickfergus F3
Carrickmacross E4
Carrigart D2
Cashel D6
Castlebar B4
Castlebellingham E4
Castleblayney E4
Castlecomer D6
Castlederg D3
Castledermot E6
Castleisland B6
Castlemaine B7
Castlepollard D4
Castlerea C4
Castletownroche C7
Castlewellan F3
Cavan D4
Ceanannus Mór E4
Charlestown C4
Claregalway C5
Claremorris C4
Clifden B4
Cloghan D5
Clogher D3
Clonakilty B7
Clonee E5
Clones D3
Clonmel D6
Clough F3
Coalisland E3
Cobh C7
Coleraine E2
Collon E4
Cookstown E3
Cootehill D5
CORK C7
Craigavon E3
Creeslough D2
Croom C6
Crossmaglen E4
Crossmolina B3
Daingean D5
Delvin D4
Dingle A6
Donegal D3
Douglas C7
Downpatrick F3
Drimoleague B7
Drogheda E4
Dromod D4
Dromore D3
Dromore West C3
Dromore E3
Drumcollogher B6
Drumshanbo D4
Drumsna D4
DUBLIN E5
Dun Laoghaire E5
Dundalk E4
Dundonald Comber F3
Dungannon E3
Dungarvan D7
Dungiven E2
Dungloe C2
Dunlavin E5
Dunleer E4
Dunmanway B7
Dunmore C4
Dunshaughlin E5
Durrow D6
Edenderry D5
Edgeworthstown D4
Enfield E5
Ennis B5
Enniscorthy E6
Enniskillen D3
Ennistymon B5
Fahan D2
Falcarragh D2
Farranfore B7
Fenagh D4
Fermoy C7
Fethard D6
Fintona D3
Foxford B4
Foynes B6
Frenchpark C4
Galway B5
Garvagh E2
Glenariff F2
Glenbeigh A7
Glencolumbkille C2
Glengarriff B7
Glenties C2
Gorey E6
Gort C5
Granard D4
Greystones E5
Gweedore C2
Headford B4
Holywood F3
Irvinestown D3
Keady E3
Kenmare B7
Kesh D3
Kilbeggan D5
Kilcock E5
Kilcolgan C5
Kilcullen E5
Kildare E5
Kildorrey C7
Kilkee B6
Kilkeel F4
Kilkenny D6
Killaloe C6
Killarney B7
Killenaule D6
Killeshandra D4
Killmallock C6
Killorglin B7
Killyleagh F3
Kilrea E2
Kilrush B6
Kingscourt E4
Kinnegad D5
Kinsale C7
Kinvara C5
Knock C4
Knocklong C6
Knocktopher D6
Larne F2
Leighlinbridge D6
Leixlip E5
Letterfrack B4
Letterkenny D2
Limavady E2
LIMERICK C6
Lisburn F3
Lismore C7
Lisnaskea D3
Listowel B6
Londonderry D2
Longford D4
Loughrea C5
Louisburgh B4
Lucan E5
Lurgan E3
Maam Cross B4
Macroom B7
Maghera E2
Magherafelt E3
Maguiresbridge D3
Mallow C7
Manorhamilton C3
Markethill E3
Mass C2
Midleton C7
Milestone C6
Milford D2
Milltown Malbay B5
Mitchelstown C6
Moate D5
Mohil D4
Monaghan E3
Monasterevan D5
Moneymore E3
Mount Bellew C4
Mountmellick D5
Mountrath D5
Moville E2
Moycullen B5
Muff D2
Mullingar D4
Mulrany B4
Naas E5
Navan E4
Nenagh C6
New Ross D6
Newbliss D3
Newbridge E5
Newcastle West B6
Newcastle F3
Newport C6
Newport B4
Newry E3
Newtownabbey F3
Newtownards F3
Newtownhamilton E3
Newtownstewart D3
Oldcastle D4
Omagh D3
Oranmore C5
Oughterard B4
Partry B4
Patrickswell C6
Port Laoise D5
Portadown E3
Portaferry F3
Portrush E2
Portstewart E2
Portumna C5
Quigley's Point E2
Randalstown E3
Rathangan E5
Rathcoole E5
Rathcormac C7
Rathdrum E5
Rathfriland E3
Rathkeale C6
Rathluirc C6
Rathmore B7
Rathnew E6
Recess B4
Rochfortbridge D5
Roscommon C4
Roscrea D5
Rosslare Harbour E7
Rosslare E7
Roundwood E5
Saintfield F3
Schull B8
Shannon C6
Shercock E4
Sion Mills D2
Skerries E4
Skibbereen B8
Slane E4
Sligo C3
Sneem A7
Strabane D2
Stradbally D5
Strangford F3
Stranorlar D2
Swanlinbar D3
Swinford C4
Swords E5
Tallowbridge C7
Tandragee E3
Tarbert B6
Templemore D6
Thomastown D6
Thurles D6
Tipperary C6
Tralee B6
Tramore D7
Trim E4
Tuam C4
Tuamgraney C5
Tubbercurry C3
Tullamore D5
Tullow E6
Tulsk C4
Urlingford D6
Virginia D4
Warrenpoint E4
Waterford D7
Waterville A7
Westport B4
Wexford E6
Whitehead F3
Wicklow E5
Youghal C7

CORK

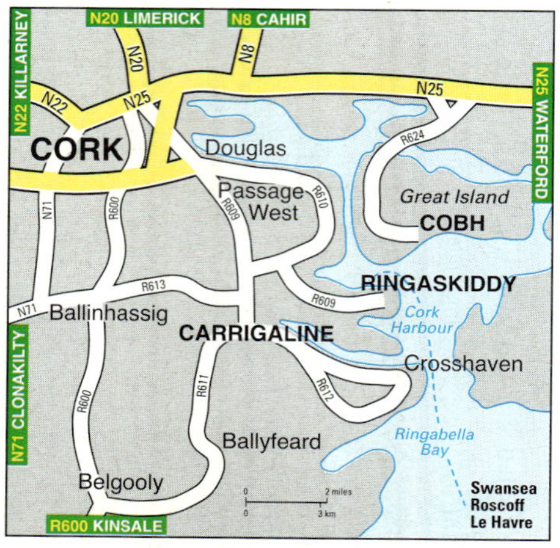

DUBLIN

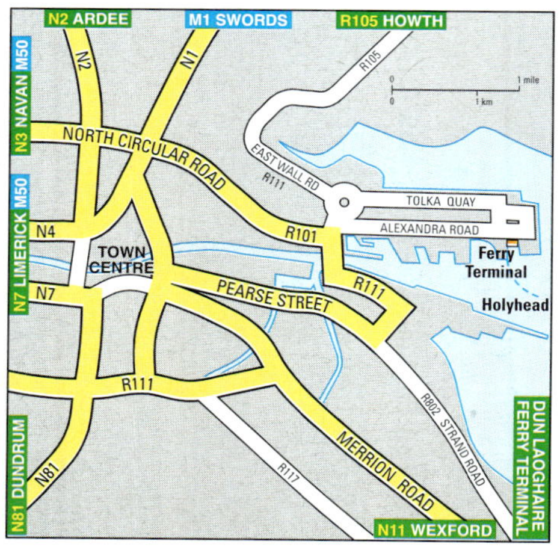

DUN LAOGHAIRE

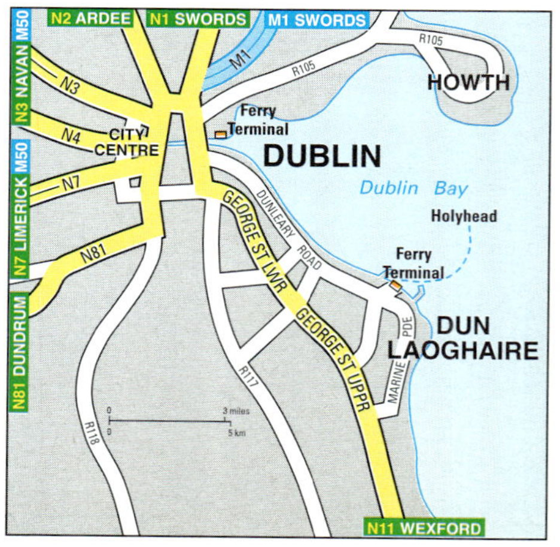

LARNE
A2 BALLYCASTLE
North Channel
TOWN CENTRE
Ferry Terminal
Larne Lough
Cairnryan
A2 CARRICKFERGUS
NORTHERN IRELAND
REPUBLIC OF IRELAND
BELFAST
DUBLIN
LIMERICK
CORK
Londonderry
Galway
Sligo
Belfast Lough
Donegal Bay
Galway Bay
Aran Islands
Dingle Bay
Dundalk Bay
Wexford Bay
St. George's Channel
ROSSLARE
N11 DUBLIN
R730 WEXFORD
Rosslare Point
Wexford Harbour
Ferry Terminal
Fishguard
Pembroke
Cherbourg
Le Havre
ROSSLARE HARBOUR
KILLINICK
TAGOAT
KILRANE
Carnsore Point
R739 KILMORE QUAY
R736 NEW ROSS
30 Kilometres
15 Miles

A
B
C
D
E
F
G
1
2
3
4
5
6
7
8
9
ISLES OF SCILLY
same scale as main map
St Helen's
White Island
Lower Town
St Martin's
Middle Town
Higher Town
Old Town
Grimsby
New Grimsby
Bryher
Tresco
Eastern Isles
Samson
North West Channel
Crow Sound
Maypole
Hugh Town
St Mary's
The Garrison
Old Town
Scilly Isles
Crim Rocks
Broad Sound
Annet
Gugh
St Agnes
Western Rocks
Smith Sound
Bishop Rock
CORNWALL
Newland
Pentire Point
Pentireglaze
New Polzeath
Gulland Rock
Gunver Head
Trevose Head
Quies
Constantine Bay
Treyarnon
St Merryn
Trevone
Padstow
Porthcothan Beach
Porthcothan
Park Head
Bedruthan Steps
Mawgan Porth
Berryl's Point
Watergate Bay
Trenance
St Mawgan
St Eval
St Ervan
Rumford
Tregurrian
Talskiddy
St Columb Major
Town Head
Newquay
Newquay Bay
Pentire
Kelsey Head
West Pentire
Holywell
Fistral Bay
Penhale Point
Ligger Pt
Ligger or Perran Bay
Perranporth
Goonhavern
St Columb Minor
Quintrell Downs
Kestle Mill
Colan
Mountjoy
St Columb Road
Retyn
Fraddon
St Enoder
Summercourt
Newlyn East
Mitchell
Carland Cross
Bawden Rocks or Man and his Man
St Agnes Head
St Agnes
Trevellas
Mithian
Bolingey
Perranzabuloe
Callestick
Zelah
St Allen
Trispen
St Erme
Tresillian
Portreath
Porthtowan
Mount Hawke
Mawla
Three Burrows
Blackwater
Chacewater
Shortlanesend
Tregavethan
Truro
Malpas
St Clement
Merther
Trewarthenick
Ruan Lanihorne
Tresillick
Philleigh
Portscatho
Gerrans
St Mawes
St Anthony
Zone Point
Greeb Point
Godrevy Island
Crane Islands
Navax Point
Gwithian
Kehelland
Illogan
Pool
Redruth
Carn Brea
St Day
Lanner
Camborne
Troon
Carharrack
Twelveheads
Baldhu
Threemilestone
Kea
Playing Place
Old Kea
St Michael Penkevil
Carn Naun Pt
The Carrack's
St Ives
St Ives Bay
The Island
Carbis Bay
Lelant
Hayle
Phillack
Connor Downs
Angarrack
Gwinear
Leedstown
Praze-an-Beeble
Crowan
Porkellis
Burras
Stithians
Ponsanooth
Perranarworthal
Devoran
Carnon Downs
Feock
Mylor Bridge
Mylor
Flushing
Penryn
Falmouth
FALMOUTH BAY
Pendennis Point
Maen Porth
Mawnan
Mawnan Smith
Constantine
Gweek
Helford
St Anthony
Nare Point
Manaccan
St Martin
Porthallow
Porthoustock
Manacle Point
The Manacles
Coverack
Lowland Pt
Black Head
Gurnard's Head
Zennor
Porthmeor
Pendeen Watch
Morvah
Pendeen
Lower Boscaswell
Trewellard
Botallack
Cape Cornwall
The Brisons
St Just
Kelynack
Halsetown
Towednack
Nancledra
Newbridge
Madron
Heamoor
Gulval
Penzance
Newlyn
Mousehole
St Clement's Isle
Paul
Sennen Cove
Sennen
Longships
LAND'S END
Porthcurno
St Levan
Gwennap Head
Treen
Logan Rock
Lamorna Cove
St Buryan
Boleigh
Crows-an-wra
Catchall
Kerris
Drift
Lower Drift
Sancreed
Buryas Bridge
Tredavoe
Chyandour
St Michael's Mount
Marazion
Ludgvan
Crowlas
Longrock
Perranuthnoe
Cudden Point
Praa Sands
Germoe
Ashton
Rinsey
Trewavas Head
Porthleven
Breage
Sithney
Helston
Godolphin Cross
Townshend
Relubbus
St Hilary
Goldsithney
Tregonning Hill
St Erth
St Erth Praze
Fraddam
Nancegollan
Wendron
Crowntown
MOUNT'S BAY
Gunwalloe
Berepper
Cury
Mullion
Mullion Cove
Mullion Island
Poldhu Point
Poldhu Cove
Porth Mellin
Predannack Wollas
Vellan Head
Kynance Cove
Lizard
LIZARD POINT
Landewednack
Hot Point
Cadgwith
Ruan Minor
Grade
Kuggar
Ruan Major
Gwenter
Penhale
Goonhilly Downs
Traboe
St Keverne
Newtown in St Martin
Tregidden
Garras
Mawgan
Crosslanes
CHANNEL location
A30
A39
A390
A393
A394
A3083
A3071
A3075
A3076
A3058
A3059
A392
A389
A3078
A3074
A3110

9
G
H
J
K
L
M
N
1
2
3
4
5
6
7
8
9
Widemouth Bay
Bridgerule
Holsworthy
Okehampton
Launceston
Camelford
Boscastle
Tintagel
Port Isaac
Wadebridge
Bodmin
BODMIN MOOR
Lostwithiel
Liskeard
Looe
East Looe
West Looe
St George's or Looe Island
ST AUSTELL
St Austell Bay
Fowey
Polruan
Mevagissey
Mevagissey Bay
Gorran Haven
Dodman Point
Saltash
Torpoint
PLYMOUTH
Devonport
Plympton
Ivybridge
Tavistock
Gunnislake
Callington
Princetown
DARTMOOR
NATIONAL
Whitsand Bay
Rame Head
Plymouth Sound
Eddystone Rocks
Santander (summer only)
Roscoff
ALDERNEY
The Swinge
St Anne
same scale as main map
GUERNSEY
St Peter Port
St Sampson
Herm
SARK
Little Sark
St Helier & St Malo
Pleinmont Pt
Jerbourg Pt
same scale as main map
Alderney
Herm
Sark
Jersey
same scale as main map
JERSEY
St Helier
St Aubin
St Brelade
St Ouen
St Ouen's Bay
St Catherine's Bay
Gorey
Grouville
St Martin
St John
St Peter Port & Poole
St Malo
Noirmont Pt
G
H
J
K
L
M
N

A
B
C
D
E
F
G
1
2
3
4
5
6
7
8
9
17
D E V O N
DARTMOOR
NATIONAL PARK
Crediton
Tiverton
EXETER
EXMOUTH
Budleigh Salterton
Sidmouth
Honiton
Ottery St Mary
Dawlish
Teignmouth
Newton Abbot
TORQUAY
PAIGNTON
Brixham
Dartmouth
Totnes
Ashburton
Buckfastleigh
Ivybridge
Plympton
Kingsbridge
Salcombe
Princetown
Moretonhampstead
Okehampton
Babbacombe Bay
Tor Bay
Start Bay
Bigbury Bay
Bolt Head
Prawle Point
Start Point
Berry Head
Hope's Nose
Stoke Fleming
Kingswear
Chudleigh
Bovey Tracey
Cullompton
Topsham
M5
A30
A38
A380
A385
A377
A361
A379

G
H
J
K
L
M
N
1
2
3
4
5
6
7
8
9
18
19
12
LYME BAY
D O R S E T
Yeovil
Sherborne
Ilminster
Chard
Crewkerne
Axminster
Lyme Regis
Charmouth
Bridport
Beaminster
Dorchester
WEYMOUTH
Fortuneswell
ISLE OF PORTLAND
Bill of Portland
Easton
Weston
Southwell
Grove
Chesil Beach
Portland Harbour
Weymouth Bay
Ringstead Bay
Wareham
Wool
Lulworth Cove
Blandford Forum
Sturminster Newton
Stalbridge
Maiden Newton
Cerne Abbas
Puddletown
Tolpuddle
Bere Regis
Abbotsbury
Portesham
Upwey
Broadwey
Preston
Osmington
Chickerell
Charlestown
Wyke Regis
Winterborne Abbas
West Bexington
Burton Bradstock
West Bay
Golden Cap
Evershot
Yetminster
Sydling St Nicholas
Piddletrenthide
Milborne Port
Henstridge
Merriott
South Petherton
Martock
Kingston Russell
Littlebredy
Askerswell
Puncknowle
Swyre
Bradford Peverell
Charminster
Stinsford
Broadmayne
Warmwell
Owermoigne
Winfrith Newburgh
East Lulworth
East Stoke
Bovington Camp
Moreton
Crossways
Affpuddle
Briantspuddle
Milborne St Andrew
Winterborne Kingston
Bloxworth
Milton Abbas
Winterborne Whitechurch
Winterborne Stickland
Shillingstone
Okeford Fitzpaine
Hazelbury Bryan
Mappowder
Higher Ansty
Cheselbourne
Dewlish
Melcombe Bingham
Buckland Newton
Alton Pancras
Holnest
Hermitage
Leigh
Chetnole
Stockwood
Melbury Osmond
Melbury Bubb
Halstock
Corscombe
Mosterton
Misterton
Broadwindsor
Drimpton
Blackdown
Thorncombe
Hawkchurch
Marshwood
Wootton Fitzpaine
Uplyme
Musbury
Whitchurch Canonicorum
Symondsbury
Chideock
Netherbury
Loders
Powerstock
Toller Porcorum
Toller Fratrum
Frampton
Compton Valence
Grimstone
Stratton
Frome St Quentin
Chalmington
Cattistock
Minterne Magna
Godmanstone
Nether Cerne
Forston
Piddlehinton
Puddletown Forest
Tincleton
Woodsford
Lower Bockhampton
West Stafford
West Knighton
Poxwell
Sutton Poyntz
Bincombe
Martinstown
Winterborne Monkton
Winterborne Steepleton
Holworth
Chaldon Herring or East Chaldon
West Lulworth
Lulworth Camp
Tyneham
Kimmeridge
Steeple
Church Knowle
Creech
Grange Heath
Holme Bridge
Sandford
Ridge
Stoborough
Slepe
Lytchett Matravers
Morden
Anderson
Winterborne Zelston
Spetisbury
Charlton Marshall
Tarrant Crawford
Tarrant Keyneston
Tarrant Rushton
Tarrant Rawston
Tarrant Monkton
Tarrant Launceston
Tarrant Hinton
Tarrant Gunville
Pimperne
Stourpaine
Durweston
Iwerne Courtney or Shroton
Iwerne Minster
Child Okeford
Hammoon
Manston
Hinton St Mary
Marnhull
Todber
Stour Row
Fontmell Magna
Sutton Waldron
Compton Abbas
Melbury Abbas
Cann Common
Twyford
Stubhampton
Farnham
Chettle
Ashmore
Tollard Royal
Danger Zone
South West Coast Path
A35
A30
A37
A352
A354
A356
A357
A358
A350
A351
A3066
A3030
A303
A31

A
B
C
D
E
F
G
1
2
3
4
5
6
7
8
9
20
19
11
Bradford-on-Avon
Devizes
Trowbridge
Westbury
Frome
Warminster
SALISBURY PLAIN
WILTSHIRE
Amesbury
ANDOVER
Ludgershall
North Tidworth
SALISBURY
Wilton
Shaftesbury
Gillingham
Mere
Romsey
SOUTHAMPTON
Blandford Forum
Wimborne Minster
Ringwood
Fordingbridge
THE NEW FOREST
Lyndhurst
Brockenhurst
Lymington
POOLE
Poole Harbour
Poole Bay
BOURNEMOUTH
CHRISTCHURCH
Christchurch Bay
Wareham
Swanage
ISLE OF PURBECK
Studland Bay
Milford on Sea
Totland
The Needles
St Aldhelm's or St Alban's Head
Durlston Head
Hengistbury Head
Cherbourg
Guernsey & Jersey
DORSET
HAMPSHIRE

G
H
J
K
L
M
N
1
2
3
4
5
6
7
8
9
14
21
BASINGSTOKE
FLEET
FARNBOROUGH
ALDERSHOT
FARNHAM
GUILDFORD
WOKING
CAMBERLEY
FRIMLEY
Godalming
Haslemere
Alton
Petersfield
Midhurst
Petworth
Arundel
CHICHESTER
HAVANT
FAREHAM
GOSPORT
PORTSMOUTH
PORTSMOUTH CITY
BOGNOR REGIS
Littlehampton
Middleton-on-Sea
Selsey
Selsey Bill
RYDE
Newport
Cowes
East Cowes
Sandown
Shanklin
Ventnor
Bembridge
St Catherine's Point
OF WIGHT
S O L E N T
W E S T
Sandown Bay
Culver Cliff
Bembridge Foreland
Santander (winter only)
Bilbao
St Malo
Cherbourg
Caen and Le Havre
M3
M27
M275
M25
A3(M)
A3
A31
A27
A259
A272
A286
A29
A24
A339
A30
A325
A287
A32
A283
A281
A285
A3055
A3054
A3020
A3021
Alice Holt Forest
Forest of Bere
Bracklesham Bay
Portsmouth Harbour
Langstone Harbour
Chichester Harbour
Hayling Island
Thorney Island
Emsworth
Havant
Waterlooville
Bishop's Waltham
Wickham
Titchfield
Hamble-le-Rice
Lee-on-the-Solent
Stubbington
Southsea
Eastney
West Wittering
East Wittering
Bosham
Worthing
Goring-by-Sea
Ferring
Rustington
Angmering
Storrington
Pulborough
Billingshurst
Cranleigh
Liphook
Grayshott
Hindhead
Milford
Witley
Chiddingfold
Liss
Bordon
New Alresford
Chawton
Medstead
Four Marks
Odiham
Hook
Tadley
Kingsclere
Overton
Whitchurch
Sutton Scotney
Kings Worthy
Chandler's Ford
Eastleigh
Fishbourne
Brading
Godshill
Rookley
Wroxall
Niton
Chale
Brighstone
Yarmouth

EPSOM
BANSTEAD
LEATHERHEAD
DORKING
REIGATE
Redhill
Caterham
Warlingham
Oxted
Sevenokes
TONBRIDGE
ROYAL TUNBRIDGE WELLS
Southborough
CRAWLEY
HORSHAM
East Grinstead
Haywards Heath
Cuckfield
Burgess Hill
Lewes
Hailsham
EASTBOURNE
BRIGHTON
HOVE
BRIGHTON & HOVE
WORTHING
Shoreham-by-Sea
Portslade by-Sea
Southwick
Newhaven
Seaford
Peacehaven
Crowborough
Uckfield
Heathfield
Wadhurst
Edenbridge
Lingfield
Horley
Billingshurst
Steyning
Lancing
Beachy Head
Pevensey Bay
Dieppe
ASHDOWN FOREST
SURREY
WEST SUSSEX
EAST SUSSEX
KENT
SOUTH DOWNS
M25
M23
M26
A B C D E F G
1 2 3 4 5 6 7 8 9

CHANNEL TUNNEL MAPS

Le Shuttle: Access from the UK

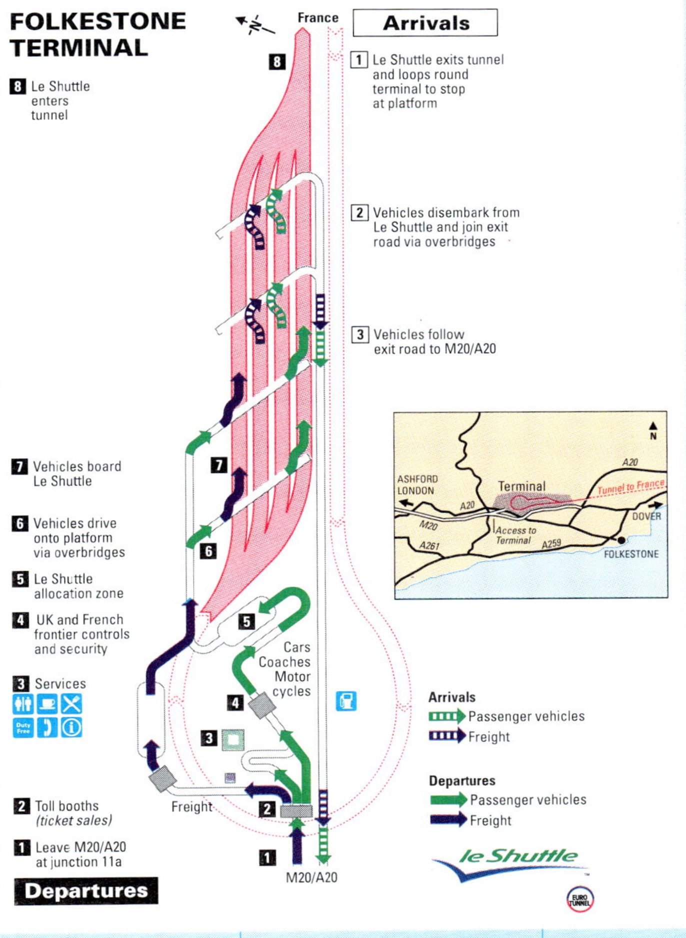

Le Shuttle: Access from France

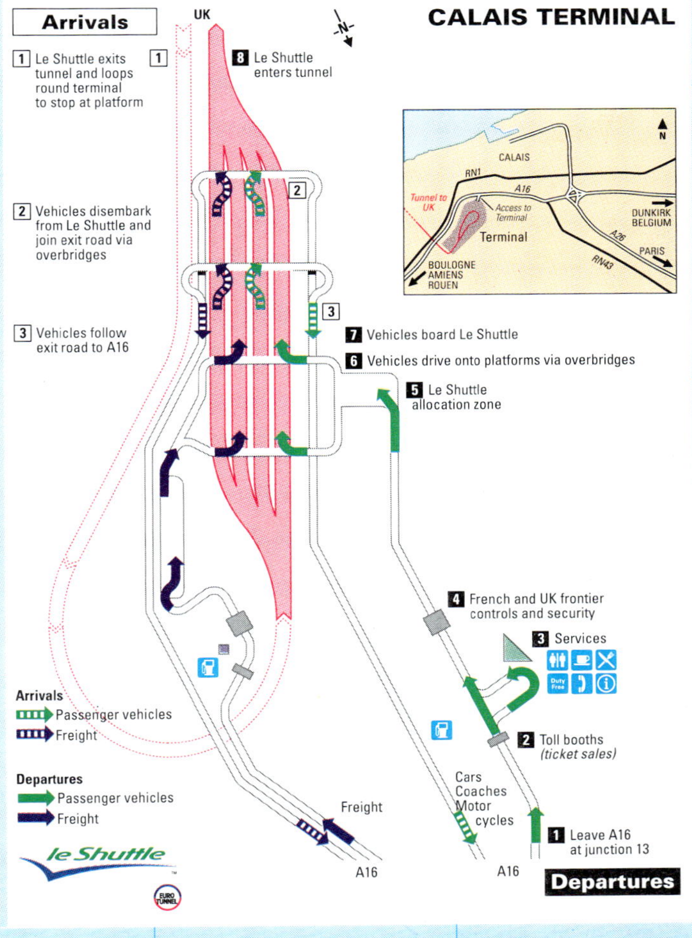

A
B
24
C
D
E
25
F
G
1
2
3
4
5
6
7
8
9
SWANSEA
PORT TAL
SWANSEA BAY
Burry Holms
Llanmadoc
Llangennith
Rhossili Bay
Rhossili Down
Rhossili
Worms Head
Middleton
Llanddewi
Reynoldston
Fairyhill
Oldwalls
Llanrhidian
Knelston
A4118
B4247
Penrice
Oxwich
Port Eynon
Overton
Port Eynon Point
Horton
Port Eynon Bay
Oxwich Green
Oxwich Bay
Cefn Bryn
Penmaen
Nicholaston
Ilston
Parkmill
Pennard
Pwlldu Head
Bishopston
Newton
The Mumbles
Mumbles Head
Black Pill
West Cross
A4067
A483
Killay
Sketty
Oystermouth
Cork (summer only)
North West Point
LUNDY
Rat Island
Shutter Rock
BARNSTAPLE
OR
BIDEFORD BAY
Haddon's Mouth
The Valley of Rocks
Woody Bay
Trentishoe
Martinhoe
Widmouth Head
Ilfracombe
Bull Point
Lee
Slade
Combe Martin
Berrynarbor
Mortehoe
Morte Point
Rockham Bay
Woolacombe
Morte Bay
Mullacott Cross
B3230
B3343
Trimstone
West Down
Sterridge
A399
A3123
Berry Down Cross
East Down
Patchole
Kentisbury
Kentisbury Ford
Blackmoor Gate
Churchtown
Challacombe Common
Challacombe
Parracombe
Heale
A39
Baggy Point
Croyde Bay
Croyde
Georgeham
Pickwell
North Buckland
A361
Bittadon
Halsinger
Knowle
Milltown
Muddiford
Arlington
Arlington Beccott
Loxhore
Knightacott
Bratton Fleming
Shoulsbarrow Common
Saunton
Saunton Sands
Braunton
Braunton Burrows
Danger Zone
Pippacott
Marwood
Prixford
Heanton Punchardon
Wrafton
Ashford
Kings Heanton
Shirwell
Shirwell Cross
Goodleigh
Stoke Rivers
Benton
Lydcott
Brayford
High Bray
Heasley Mill
Barnstaple
Newport
Pilton
Bickington
Fremington
Yelland
Instow
Appledore
The Neck
Northam Burrows
Westward Ho!
Northam
Bideford
Westleigh
Bickleton
Tawstock
Landkey
Bishop's Tawton
Swimbridge
Swimbridge Newland
Yarnscott
West Buckland
East Buckland
Charles
Gunn
Northleigh
Filleigh
Cobbaton
Herner
Hartland Point
Titchberry
Windbury Point
Gallantry Bower
Clovelly
Hartland
Stoke
Milford
Elmscott
Edistone
Philham
Tosberry
Dyke
Clovelly Cross
B3237
B3248
Buck's Mills
Horns Cross
Fairy Cross
Abbotsham
Ford
Yeo Vale
Littleham
Landcross
Horwood
Eastleigh
East-the-Water
Lovacott
Newton Tracey
St John's Chapel
Gammaton Moor
Alverdiscott
Hiscott
Woodtown
Ensis
Chittlehampton
Hudscott
Umberleigh
Atherington
Fishley Barton
Langridge
Langridgeford
High Bickington
Chittlehamholt
Satterleigh
Warkleigh
Clapworthy
South Molton
George Nympton
Alswear
Romansleigh
King's Nympton
Head Bridge
Cadbury Barton
Kingscott
Roborough
Burrington
Northcote Manor
Elstone
Colleton Mills
Chulmleigh
Villavin
Beaford
Riddlecombe
Ashreigney
Copy Lake
Chawleigh
Ashley
Eggesford Barton
Wembworthy
Hollocombe
Dolton
Dowland
Iddesleigh
Winkleigh
Brushford Barton
Nymet Rowland
Coldridge
Lapford
East Leigh
Zeal Monachorum
Bondleigh
Broadwood Kelly
Honeychurch
Sampford Courtenay
North Tawton
Bow
Broadnymet
Nymet Tracey
Itton
Taw Green
Bell
Exbourne
Jacobstowe
Folly Gate
Week St Mary
Hatherleigh
Bassett's Cross
Monkokehampton
Hele Bridge
Meeth
Petrockstow
Huish
Heanton Satchville
Merton
Winswell
Peters Marland
Woolladon
Little Torrington
Great Torrington
Taddiport
St Giles in the Wood
Huntshaw Cross
Yarnscombe
Sherwood Green
Weare Giffard
Frithelstock
Frithelstock Stone
Monkleigh
Buckland Brewer
Parkham
Parkham Ash
Goldworthy
Cranford
Woolfardisworthy
Almiston Cross
Melbury
Powler's Piece
Ashmansworthy
Kismeldon Bridge
East Putford
West Putford
Dinworthy
Bradworthy
Brendon
Abbots Bickington
Bulkworthy
Langtree
Stibb Cross
Newton St Petrock
Shebbear
Milton Damerel
Sutcombe
Alfardisworthy
Upper Tamar Lake
Lower Tamar Lake
Soldon Cross
Youldonmoor Cross
Youldon
Holsworthy Beacon
Chilsworthy
Thornbury
Buckland Filleigh
North Town
Bradford
Sheepwash
Black Torrington
Cookbury
Brandis Corner
Dunsland Cross
Highampton
Lydacott
Graddon Moor
Halwill Forest
Halwill
Beaworthy
Northlew
Ashbury
Broadbury
Upcott
Quoditch
Holsworthy
Anvil Corner
Hollacombe
Chasty
Rydon
Pyworthy
Bridgerule
Yeomadon
Tinney
Cofcott Green
North Tamerton
Hersham
Stratton
Launcells
Launcells Cross
Grimscott
Marhamchurch
Red Post
Pancrasweek
A3072
A388
A3079
A386
A377
A39
B3254
Flexbury
Poughill
Bude
Bude Haven
BUDE BAY
Helebridge
Widemouth Bay
Titson
Week Orchard
Coppathorne
Poundstock
Treskinnick
Whitstone
Tregole
Trewint
St Gennys
Crackington Haven
Knaps Longpeak
South Hole
Welcombe
Meddon
Gooseham
Morwenstow
Eastcott
Shop
Woodford
Lower Sharpnose Point
Coombe
Taylors Cross
Kilkhampton
Stibb
Youlstone
Junction
Hartland Abbey
D
E
9

G
H
J
K
L
M
N
17
25
18
BRIDGEND
RHONDDA
CYNON TAFF
PONTYPRIDD
CAERPHILLY
NEWPORT
CARDIFF
PENARTH
BARRY
VALE OF GLAMORGAN
Cowbridge
Porthcawl
Bridgend
Clevedon
MOUTH OF THE SEVERN
WESTON-SUPER-MARE
NORTH SOMERSET
BRIDGWATER BAY
Burnham-on-Sea
Minehead
Watchet
EXMOOR
NATIONAL PARK
BRIDGWATER
SOMERSET
TAUNTON
Wellington
Tiverton
Cullompton
Honiton
Ilminster
Chard
Crewkerne
Crediton
Axminster
VALE OF TAUNTON DEANE
Steep Holm
Flat Holm
Barry Island
Sully Island
1
2
3
4
5
6
7
8
9
10
18

A
B
C
D
E
F
G
1
2
3
4
5
6
7
8
9
28
17
10
11
MERTHYR TYDFIL
BLAENAU GWENT
MONMOUTHSHIRE
TORFAEN
CAERPHILLY
RHONDDA CYNON TAFF
VALE OF GLAMORGAN
CARDIFF
NEWPORT
NORTH SOMERSET
BATH & N.E. SOMERSET
CITY & COUNTY OF BRISTOL
SOMERSET
GLOUCESTERSHIRE
MOUTH OF THE SEVERN
BRIDGWATER BAY
Merthyr Tydfil
Aberdare
Tredegar
Ebbw Vale
Blaina
Abertillery
Abersychan
Blaenavon
Pontypool
Cwmbran
Usk
Monmouth
Trefynwy
Caerleon
Chepstow
Newport
Risca
Caerphilly
Pontypridd
Bargoed
Gelligaer
Blackwood
Newbridge
Abercarn
Cardiff
Penarth
Barry
Cowbridge
Llantwit Major
Flat Holm
Steep Holm
Weston-super-Mare
Clevedon
Portishead
Avonmouth
Bristol
Keynsham
Burnham-on-Sea
Highbridge
Bridgwater
Cheddar
Wells
Glastonbury
Street
Taunton
Wellington
Watchet
Minehead
Wiveliscombe
Somerton
Shepton Mallet
M4
M5
M48
M49
M32

G
H
J
K
L
M
N
29
30
1
2
3
4
5
6
7
8
9
Stroud
Nailsworth
Cirencester
Tetbury
Malmesbury
Swindon
SWINDON
Wootton Bassett
Marlborough
Hungerford
Chippenham
Calne
Corsham
Melksham
Devizes
Bath
BATH
Bradford-on-Avon
Trowbridge
Westbury
Frome
Warminster
Radstock
Shaftesbury
Gillingham
Wincanton
Bruton
Mere
Wilton
Salisbury
SALISBURY
Amesbury
Andover
Ludgershall
Pewsey
Tidworth
Chipping Sodbury
Yate
Highworth
Faringdon
Lechlade
Fairford
Cricklade
Lambourn
S A L I S B U R Y
P L A I N
W I L T S H I R E
M4
M5
A4
A36
A303
A350
A338
A346
A419
A429
A417
A345
A360
A342
A361
A30
Danger Zone

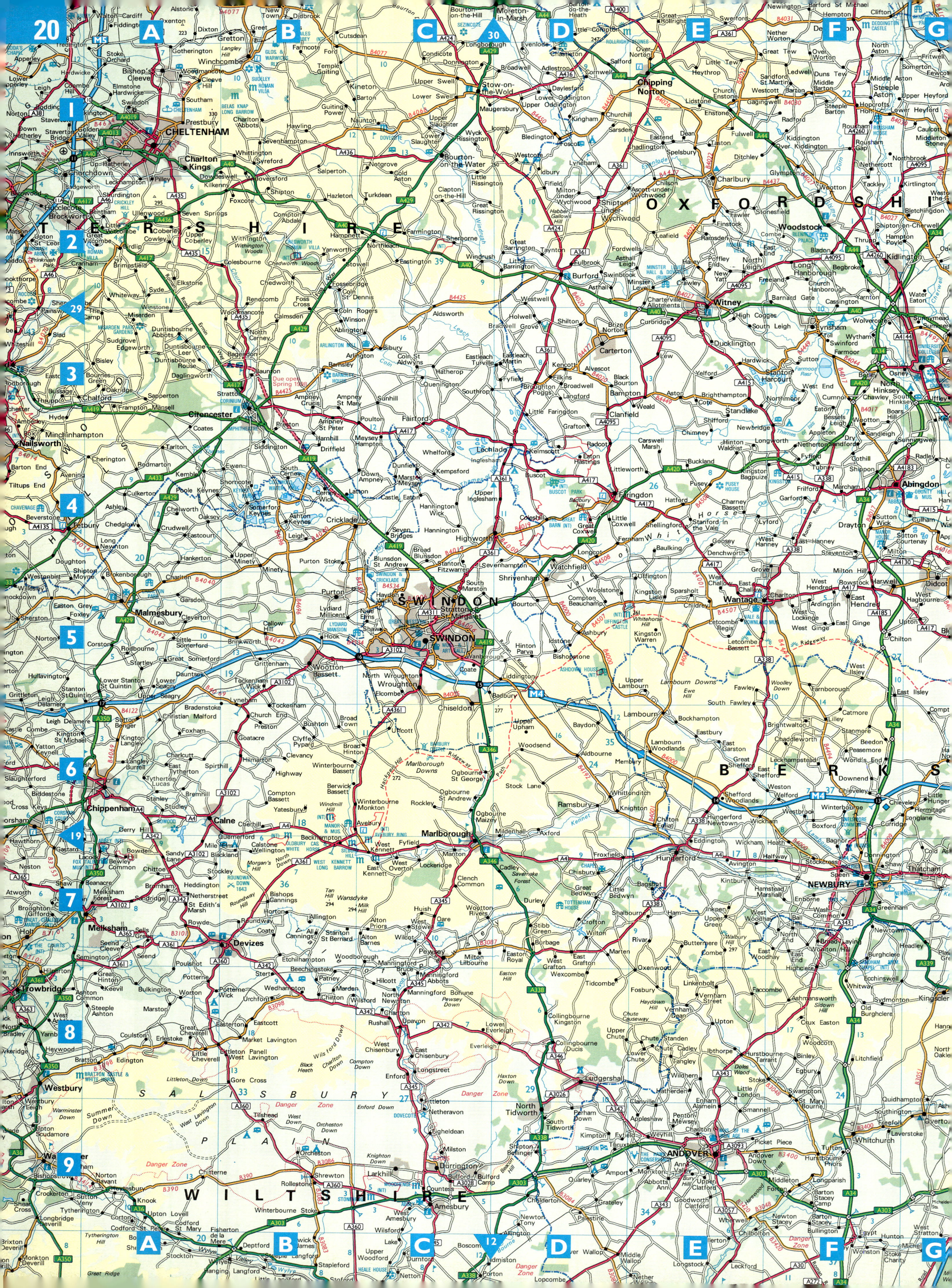
A
B
C
D
E
F
G
1
2
3
4
5
6
7
8
9
30
29
19
12
CHELTENHAM
Cheltenham
Charlton Kings
Cirencester
Nailsworth
Tetbury
Malmesbury
Chippenham
Calne
Melksham
Trowbridge
Westbury
Devizes
Marlborough
SWINDON
Swindon
Wootton Bassett
Cricklade
Highworth
Faringdon
Lechlade
Fairford
Burford
Witney
Carterton
Chipping Norton
Stow-on-the-Wold
Bourton-on-the-Water
Moreton-in-Marsh
Winchcombe
Woodstock
Kidlington
Abingdon
Wantage
Didcot
Hungerford
NEWBURY
Newbury
Thatcham
Ludgershall
Tidworth
North Tidworth
Andover
Amesbury
Durrington
Lambourn
Pewsey
Shefford Woodlands
OXFORDSHIRE
BERKS
WILTSHIRE
SALISBURY PLAIN
GLOUCESTERSHIRE
Danger Zone
M4
M5
A34
A338
A346
A350
A420
A429

G
H
J
K
L
M
N
1
2
3
4
5
6
7
8
9
BUCKINGHAMSHIRE
Bicester
AYLESBURY
LEIGHTON BUZZARD
DUNSTABLE
LUTON
HITCHIN
STEVENAGE
HARPENDEN
HEMEL HEMPSTEAD
ST ALBANS
Berkhamsted
Tring
Thame
Wendover
CHESHAM
Princes Risborough
Amersham
WATFORD
RICKMANSWORTH
HIGH WYCOMBE
Beaconsfield
Marlow
HARROW
HILLINGDON
MAIDENHEAD
SLOUGH
Henley-on-Thames
Wallingford
READING
WINDSOR
Eton
HOUNSLOW
EALING
HAMMERSMITH & FULHAM
RICHMOND UPON THAMES
KINGSTON UPON THAMES
STAINES
Wokingham
BRACKNELL
Chertsey
Weybridge
WALTON-ON-THAMES
ESHER
EPSOM
CAMBERLEY
FRIMLEY
WOKING
FARNBOROUGH
FLEET
ALDERSHOT
GUILDFORD
LEATHERHEAD
DORKING
BASINGSTOKE
FARNHAM
Godalming
Alton
BARNET
M40
M4
M25
M3
M1
A1(M)
A404(M)
A329(M)
S U R R E Y
G R E A T E R
H E R T F O R D

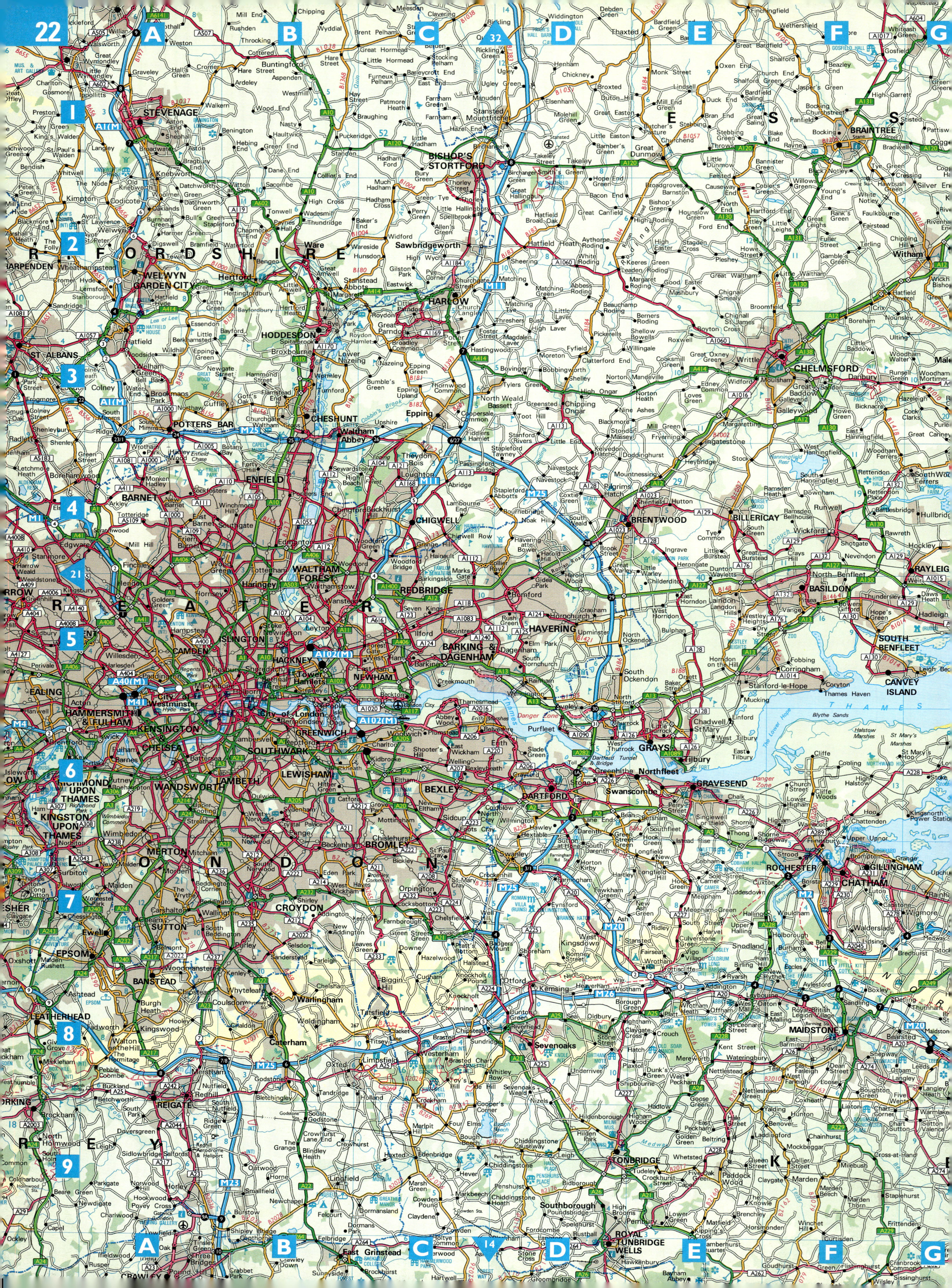

A
B
C
32
D
E
F
G
1
2
3
4
5
6
7
8
9
21
14
STEVENAGE
BISHOP'S STORTFORD
BRAINTREE
HARPENDEN
WELWYN GARDEN CITY
Hertford
Ware
Sawbridgeworth
HARLOW
Witham
ST. ALBANS
HODDESDON
CHELMSFORD
POTTERS BAR
CHESHUNT
Waltham Abbey
Epping
BARNET
ENFIELD
CHIGWELL
BRENTWOOD
BILLERICAY
RAYLEIGH
WALTHAM FOREST
REDBRIDGE
Romford
HAVERING
BASILDON
HACKNEY
ISLINGTON
CAMDEN
NEWHAM
BARKING & DAGENHAM
SOUTH BENFLEET
CANVEY ISLAND
EALING
HAMMERSMITH & FULHAM
KENSINGTON & CHELSEA
Westminster
City of London
SOUTHWARK
GREENWICH
LEWISHAM
Purfleet
GRAYS
Tilbury
RICHMOND UPON THAMES
WANDSWORTH
LAMBETH
BEXLEY
DARTFORD
Swanscombe
Northfleet
GRAVESEND
KINGSTON UPON THAMES
MERTON
BROMLEY
ROCHESTER
GILLINGHAM
CHATHAM
SUTTON
CROYDON
EPSOM
BANSTEAD
LEATHERHEAD
Warlingham
Caterham
Sevenoaks
MAIDSTONE
REIGATE
TONBRIDGE
Southborough
ROYAL TUNBRIDGE WELLS
East Grinstead
CRAWLEY
HERTFORDSHIRE
ESSEX
GREATER LONDON
SURREY
KENT
THAMES
M25
M11
M1
M20
M26
M23
M2
A1(M)

G
H
J
K
L
M
N
Hamburg
Hoek van Holland
Harwich
Dovercourt
Landguard Point
Manningtree
Mistley
Lawford
Wrabness
Parkeston
Colchester
Wivenhoe
Walton on the Naze
The Naze
Stone Point
Frinton-on-Sea
Sandy Point
Holland-on-Sea
Clacton-on-Sea
Brightlingsea
St Osyth
Jaywick
Seawick
Colne Point
Gunfleet Sand
West Mersea
Mersea Island
East Mersea
Tollesbury
Tiptree
Blackwater
Bradwell Waterside
Bradwell-on-Sea
Sales Point
St Peter's Flat
Dengie Flat
Tillingham
Dengie
Asheldham
Southminster
Dengie Marshes
Ray Sand
Maylandsea
Steeple
St Lawrence
Latchingdon
Althorne
Burnham-on-Crouch
Foulness Sands
Foulness Point
Holliwell Point
Wallasea Island
Paglesham Churchend
Paglesham Eastend
Potton Island
Foulness Island
Courtsend
Churchend
Danger Zone
Rochford
Great Wakering
Little Wakering
Havengore Island
Maplin Sands
Southend-on-Sea
Shoeburyness
Shoebury Ness
Isle of Grain
Sheerness
Queenborough
Minster
Eastchurch
Warden
Warden Point
Leysdown-on-Sea
Isle of Sheppey
Shell Ness
Sittingbourne
Faversham
Whitstable
Herne Bay
Reculver
Birchington
Westgate on Sea
Margate
South Channel
Long Nose Spit
Foreness Point
Cliftonville
White Ness
North Foreland
Broadstairs
Isle of Thanet
Ramsgate
Oostende
Dunkerque
Pegwell Bay
Sandwich Bay
Sandwich
Canterbury
Sturry
Minster
Deal
Walmer
Kingsdown
St Margaret's at Cliffe
St Margaret's Bay
South Foreland
Dover
Ashford
Folkestone
Calais
Channel
East Wear Bay
M2
M20
A2
A20
A28
A299
A256
A258
A257
A12
A120
A133
A13

A
B
C
D
E
F
G
1
2
3
4
5
6
7
8
9
PEMBROKESHIRE COAST
NATIONAL PARK
PEMBROKESHIRE
ST BRIDE'S
BAY
CARMARTHEN
BAY
Cardigan Island
Cemaes Head
Cardigan
St Dogmaels
Newcastle Emlyn
Newport
Newport Bay
Dinas Head
Fishguard Bay
Fishguard
Goodwick
Strumble Head
Rosslare
St David's
St David's Head
Ramsey Island
Skomer Island
Skokholm Island
St Ann's Head
Dale
Milford Haven
MILFORD HAVEN
Neyland
Pembroke
Pembroke Dock
Haverfordwest
Narberth
Whitland
St Clears
Saundersfoot
Tenby
Caldey Island
St Govan's Head
Stackpole Head
Freshwater West
Angle
Solva
Newgale
Broad Haven
Little Haven
Crymych
Mynydd Preseli
Laugharne
Pendine
Amroth
Kilgetty
Begelly
Manorbier
Penally
Lamphey
Carew
Cork (summer only)

G
H
J
K
L
M
N
26
CEREDIGION
POWYS
CARMARTHENSHIRE
SWANSEA
NEATH PORT TALBOT
AFAN FOREST PARK
BRIDGEND
RHONDDA CYNON TAF
MERTHYR
VALE OF GLAMORGAN
BRECON BEACONS NATIONAL PARK
FOREST FAWR
MOUNTAIN ASH
SWANSEA BAY
Aberaeron
New Quay
Llanarth
Lampeter
Llanwrtyd Wells
Builth Wells
Llandovery
Llandeilo
Ammanford
Carmarthen
Kidwelly (Cydweli)
Burry Port
LLANELLI
Gorseinon
SWANSEA
The Mumbles
Mumbles Head
Port Eynon
Rhossili
Worms Head
Oxwich
NEATH
PORT TALBOT
MAESTEG
Pontycymer
Bridgend
Porthcawl
Aberdare
Treorchy
Pontypridd
Ystradgynlais
Pontardawe
Glanaman
Brynamman
Pontardulais
Llandysul
Newcastle Emlyn
Talgarreg
Sennybridge
Trecastle
Glyncorrwg
Tonypandy
Cowbridge
St Athan
Nash Point
Tusker Rock
Southerndown
Ogmore-by-Sea
Danger Zone
Burry Holms
Whitford Point
Llanrhidian Sands
Cefn Sidan Sands
Pembrey Forest
Llyn Brianne
M4
A40
A48
A483
A465
A470
A4067
A4109
A4069
28
1
2
3
4
5
6
7
8
9
16
17
18

Nefyn
Pistyll
Llithfaen
Morfa Nefyn
Edern
Tudweiliog
Porth Colmon
Llangwnnadl
Methlem
Aberdaron
Pen y Cil
Abersoch
Llanbedrog
Pwllheli
Criccieth
Porthmadog
Ffestiniog
Penrhyndeudraeth
Minffordd
Porthmeirion
Trawsfynydd
Talsarnau
Harlech
TREMADOC BAY
SNOWDONIA
NATIONAL
PARK
G W Y N E D D
COED Y BRENIN FOREST PARK
Llanbedr
Dyffryn Ardudwy
Barmouth
BARMOUTH BAY
Fairbourne
Dolgellau
Cadair Idris
Llwyngwril
Tywyn
Aberdyfi
Machynlleth
Corris
Borth
C A R D I G A N
B A Y
Aberystwyth
Bow Street
Devil's Bridge
Llanrhystud
Aberaeron
New Quay
C E R E D I G I O N
Tregaron
Lampeter
Llandysul
Synod Inn
Cardigan Island

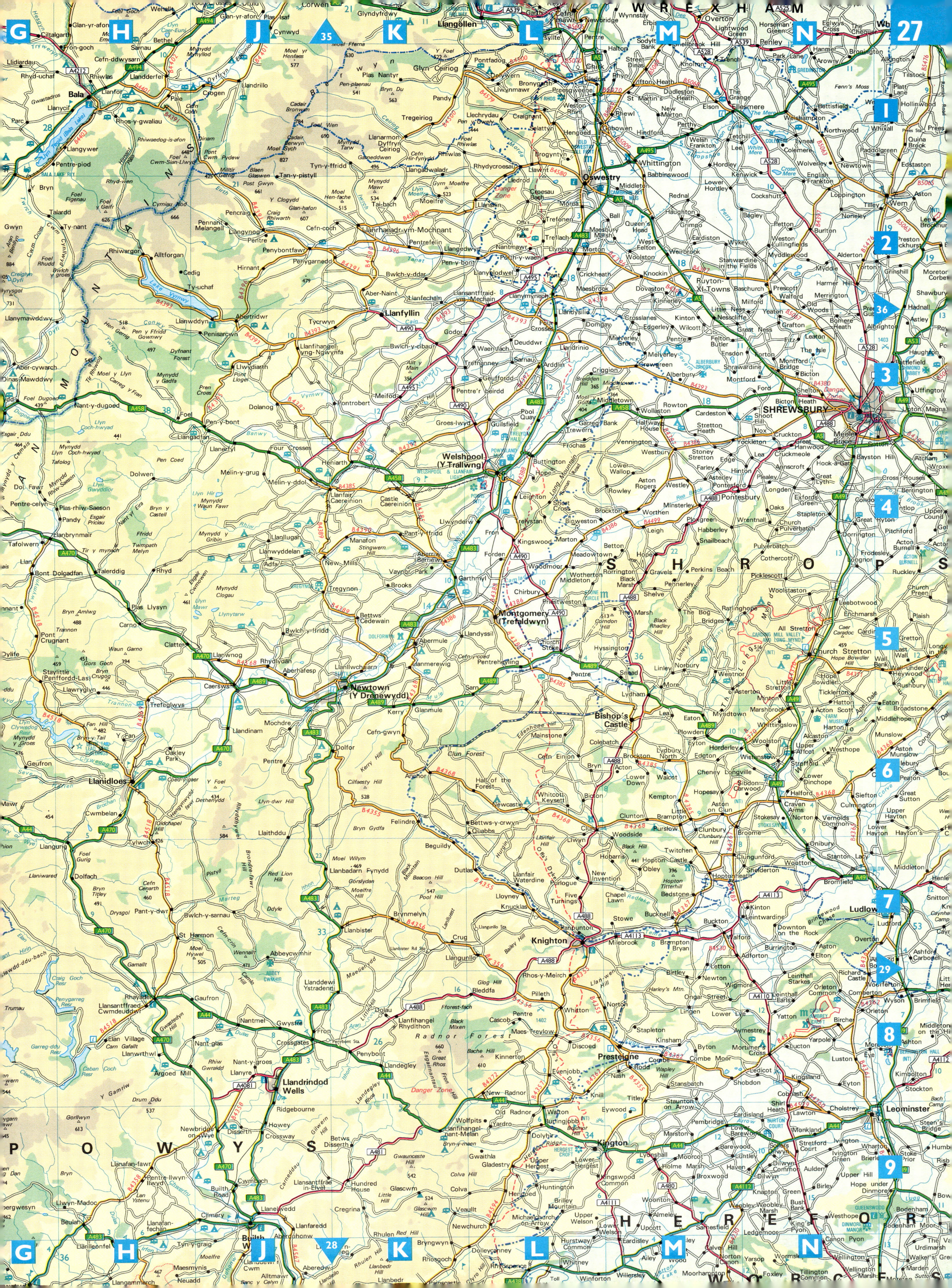
WREXHAM
SHROPS
POWYS
HEREFORD
BERWYN
ARAN MOUNTAINS
Llangollen
Bala
Oswestry
Ellesmere
Wem
Shrewsbury
Welshpool (Y Trallwng)
Llanfyllin
Montgomery (Trefaldwyn)
Newtown (Y Drenewydd)
Llanidloes
Bishop's Castle
Church Stretton
Craven Arms
Clun
Ludlow
Knighton
Presteigne
Kington
Leominster
Rhayader
Llandrindod Wells
Builth Wells
Llanwrtyd
Corwen
Whitchurch
Pontesbury
Minsterley
Caersws
Llanbrynmair
Llanfair Caereinion
Llangynog
Lake Vyrnwy
New Radnor
Radnor Forest
Clee Hill
Long Mynd
Wenlock Edge
Offa's Dyke
Danger Zone
G H J K L M N
35
36
28
29
2
3
4
5
6
7
8
9
i

A
B
C
D
E
F
G
1
2
3
4
5
6
7
8
9
27
26
25
18
Newtown (Y Drenewydd)
Llanidloes
Rhayader
Llandrindod Wells
Builth Wells
Llanwrtyd Wells
Knighton
Presteigne
Kington
Hay-on-Wye
Brecon
Talgarth
Crickhowell
Abergavenny
Merthyr Tydfil
Tredegar
Ebbw Vale
Blaenau Gwent
Blaina
Blaenavon
Abertillery
Pontypool
Aberdare
Bishop's Castle
Clun
Craven Arms
P O W Y S
H E R E
Radnor Forest
Black Mountains
Brecon Beacons
Brecon Beacons National Park
Fforest Fawr
Monmouths
Neath Port Talbot
Afan Forest Park
Bargoed
Gelligaer
Blackwood
Newbridge
Nantyglo
Llandovery
Trecastle
Sennybridge
Llangammarch Wells
Beulah
Llanbister
New Radnor
Old Radnor
Llyswen
Llangorse
Bwlch
Glyncorrwg
Ystradgynlais
Hirwaun
Rhayader
St Harmon
Elan Village
Pant Mawr
Dolfor
Kerry
Caersws

G
H
J
K
L
M
N
1
2
3
4
5
6
7
8
9
BIRMINGHAM
WEST BROMWICH
DUDLEY
STOURBRIDGE
HALESOWEN
WARLEY
KIDDERMINSTER
BROMSGROVE
REDDITCH
Ludlow
Bewdley
Stourport on-Severn
Droitwich
WORCESTER
Leominster
HEREFORD
Bromyard
GREAT MALVERN
Ledbury
Tewkesbury
Evesham
CHELTENHAM
GLOUCESTER
Ross-on-Wye
Monmouth (Trefynwy)
Stroud
Cirencester
Charlton Kings
Newent
Upton upon Severn
Pershore
Alcester
HEREFORD & WORCESTER
W E S T M I D L A N D S
G L O S
DEAN FOREST
AND WYE VALLEY
Forest of Dean
Wyre Forest
M5
M50
M42
30
36
19

A
B
C
D
E
F
G
37
29
20
1
2
3
4
5
6
7
8
9
WEST MIDLANDS
WARWICKSHIRE
OXFORDSHIRE
NORT
SHIRE
WEST BROMWICH
BIRMINGHAM
SOLIHULL
NUNEATON
BEDWORTH
COVENTRY
RUGBY
Kenilworth
ROYAL LEAMINGTON SPA
Warwick
REDDITCH
Daventry
Stratford-upon-Avon
Evesham
BANBURY
Brackley
Chipping Norton
Bicester
Woodstock
Witney
OXFORD
CHELTENHAM
Cirencester
Stow-on-the-Wold
Moreton-in-Marsh
Chipping Campden
Burford
Abingdon
M5
M6
M42
M40
M45
M1
M69
A38(M)

G
H
J
K
L
M
N
38
21
32
1
2
3
4
5
6
7
8
9
NORTHAMPTONSHIRE
CAMBRIDGESHIRE
MILTON KEYNES
BEDFORDSHIRE
BUCKINGHAMSHIRE
HERTFORDSHIRE
Market Harborough
CORBY
KETTERING
Oundle
Thrapston
Desborough
Rothwell
Burton Latimer
Raunds
WELLINGBOROUGH
Irthlingborough
Higham Ferrers
Rushden
NORTHAMPTON
Huntingdon
Godmanchester
St Ives
St. Neots
Ramsey
Sawtry
Olney
Newport Pagnell
Wolverton
Stony Stratford
MILTON KEYNES
Bletchley
Buckingham
BEDFORD
Kempston
Sandy
Biggleswade
Ampthill
Flitwick
LETCHWORTH
Baldock
HITCHIN
STEVENAGE
LEIGHTON BUZZARD
DUNSTABLE
LUTON
HARPENDEN
WELWYN GARDEN CITY
Hertford
AYLESBURY
Tring
Berkhamsted
HEMEL HEMPSTEAD
ST ALBANS
Thame
Wendover
CHESHAM
WATFORD
POTTERS BAR
ENFIELD

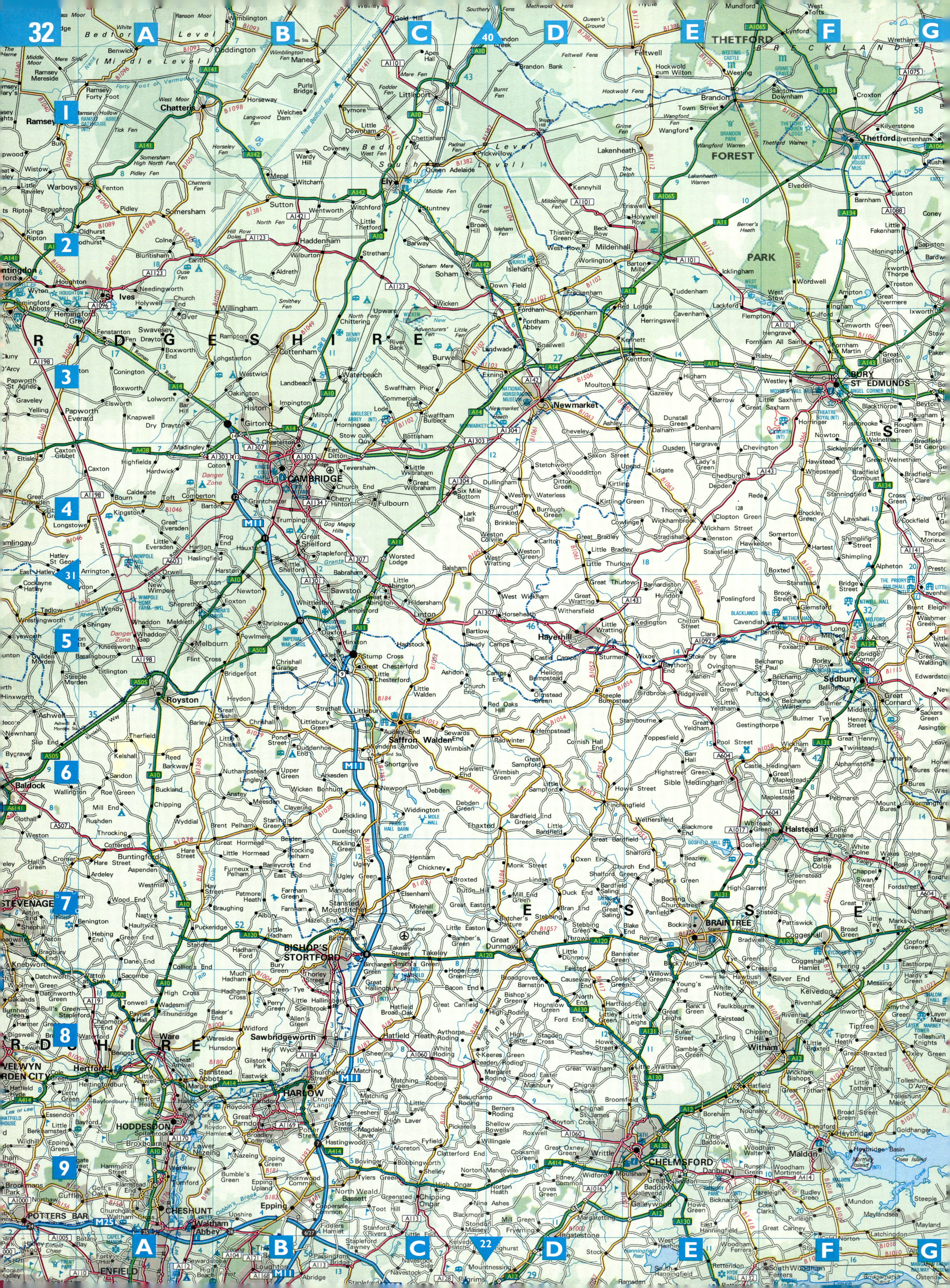
A
B
C
D
E
F
G
1
2
3
4
5
6
7
8
9
40
31
22
THETFORD
FOREST
PARK
Thetford
Brandon
Mildenhall
Ely
Ramsey
Chatteris
St Ives
Huntingdon
Newmarket
BURY ST EDMUNDS
CAMBRIDGE
Royston
Haverhill
Saffron Walden
Sudbury
Halstead
Braintree
BISHOP'S STORTFORD
Great Dunmow
STEVENAGE
HARLOW
Hertford
Ware
HODDESDON
CHESHUNT
Waltham Abbey
POTTERS BAR
ENFIELD
Epping
CHELMSFORD
Witham
Maldon
Coggeshall
Baldock
Sawbridgeworth
Ongar
Kelvedon
Lakenheath
Soham
Burwell
Linton
Clare
Thaxted
Stansted Mountfitchet
Welwyn Garden City

LOWESTOFT
Beccles
Bungay
Halesworth
Southwold
Walberswick
Dunwich
Leiston
Thorpeness
Aldeburgh
Saxmundham
Framlingham
Wickham Market
Woodbridge
Orford
Orford Ness
IPSWICH
FELIXSTOWE
Felixstowe Ferry
Harwich
Dovercourt
Walton on the Naze
Frinton-on-Sea
Holland-on-Sea
CLACTON-ON-SEA
Brightlingsea
West Mersea
Wivenhoe
Manningtree
Hadleigh
Stowmarket
Needham Market
Eye
Diss
Harleston
Kessingland
Göteborg
Esbjerg
Hamburg
Hoek van Holland
G
H
J
K
L
M
N
41
23
1
2
3
4
5
6
7
8
9

A
B
C
D
E
F
G
1
2
3
4
5
6
7
8
9
ISLE OF ANGLESEY
HOLYHEAD BAY
HOLY ISLAND
Holyhead (Caergybi)
Amlwch
Llangefni
Beaumaris
Menai Bridge
Bangor
Caernarfon
CAERNARFON BAY
CONWY BAY
Penmaenmawr
Llanfairfechan
Bethesda
Llanberis
Snowdon (Yr Wyddfa)
Capel Curig
Blaenau Ffestiniog
Ffestiniog
Porthmadog
Criccieth
Pwllheli
Nefyn
Abersoch
Aberdaron
Bardsey Island
Bardsey Sound
TREMADOC BAY
Harlech
Barmouth
BARMOUTH BAY
Dolgellau
GWYNEDD
LLEYN PENINSULA
Dublin & Dún Laoghaire
Puffin Island (Priestholm)
Great Orme
26

G
H
J
K
42
L
M
N
1
2
3
4
5
36
6
7
8
9
27
CROSBY
BOOTLE
WALLASEY
LIVERPOOL
BIRKENHEAD
MERSEYSIDE
Hoylake
West Kirby
BEBINGTON
ELLESMERE PORT
Heswall
Neston
Belfast
West Hoyle Bank
Point of Ayr
Prestatyn
RHYL
Abergele
COLWYN BAY
Llandudno
Little Ormes Head
Penrhyn Bay
Rhos-on-Sea
Llandrillo-yn-Rhos
Mostyn Quay
Holywell
Flint
FLINTSHIRE
Connah's Quay
St Asaph (Llanelwy)
Denbigh
DENBIGHSHIRE
CONWY
Llanrwst
Mold
Buckley
CHESTER
Ruthin
WREXHAM
Llangollen
Corwen
Bala
Oswestry
Llanfyllin
Welshpool (Y Trallwng)
Lake Vyrnwy
Whittington
SHREWSBURY
Mostyn Bank
Mostyn
Wrexham

A
B
C
D
E
F
G
1
2
3
4
5
6
7
8
9
44
35
27
29
ELLESMERE PORT
RUNCORN
WILMSLOW
Neston
Knutsford
Northwich
Bollington
Macclesfield
CHESTER
DELAMERE FOREST
C H E S H I R E
Winsford
Middlewich
Congleton
Sandbach
Biddulph
CREWE
Alsager
KIDSGROVE
Nantwich
NEWCASTLE-UNDER-LYME
STOKE-ON-TRENT
WREXHAM
W R E X H A M
Whitchurch
Market Drayton
Stone
Oswestry
Ellesmere
S T A F F O
SHREWSBURY
Newport
Wellington
TELFORD
S H R O P S H I R E
WOLVERHAMPTON
BRIDGNORTH
Bishop's Castle
Church Stretton
Buckley
Shotton
Connah's Quay
Mold
Llangollen
Ruabon
Hanford
Sedgley
Dudley

G
H
J
K
L
M
N
45
46
1
2
3
4
5
6
7
8
9
38
30
PEAK
DISTRICT
NATIONAL
PARK
D E R B Y
D E R B Y S H I R E
D S H I R E
NOTTS
L E I C E S T E R
WORKSOP
Buxton
Bakewell
CHESTERFIELD
Staveley
Bolsover
Dronfield
MANSFIELD WOODHOUSE
MANSFIELD
SUTTON-IN-ASHFIELD
KIRKBY IN ASHFIELD
ALFRETON
MATLOCK
Wirksworth
Ashbourne
Uttoxeter
Ripley
BELPER
HEANOR
HUCKNALL
Eastwood
ILKESTON
NOTTINGHAM
West Bridgford
Carlton
Beeston
Stapleford
LONG EATON
DERBY
BURTON UPON TRENT
SWADLINCOTE
Ashby-de-la-Zouch
COALVILLE
LOUGHBOROUGH
Shepshed
LICHFIELD
RUGELEY
TAMWORTH
BROWNHILLS
ALDRIDGE
BLOXWICH
WALSALL
SUTTON COLDFIELD
WEST BROMWICH
BIRMINGHAM
Atherstone
NUNEATON
BEDWORTH
HINCKLEY
LEICESTER
WIGSTON
Oadby
Market Warsop
M1
M42
M69
M6

NOTTINGHAM
LEICESTERSHIRE
NORTHAMPTON
DERBY
RUTL
MATLOCK
Wirksworth
ALFRETON
KIRKBY IN ASHFIELD
SUTTON IN ASHFIELD
MANSFIELD
MANSFIELD WOODHOUSE
Market Warsop
Ollerton
NEWARK-ON-TRENT
HUCKNALL
Ripley
BELPER
HEANOR
Eastwood
ILKESTON
NOTTINGHAM
Arnold
Carlton
West Bridgford
Beeston
Stapleford
LONG EATON
Clifton
Bingham
GRANTHAM
SWADLINCOTE
Ashby de la Zouch
COALVILLE
LOUGHBOROUGH
Shepshed
Melton Mowbray
Oakham
LEICESTER
Wigston
Oadby
HINCKLEY
NUNEATON
BEDWORTH
COVENTRY
Market Harborough
CORBY
KETTERING
Desborough
Uppingham
Lutterworth
Rugby
A
B
C
D
E
F
G
1
2
3
4
5
6
7
8
9
M1
M69
M6

G
H
J
K
L
M
N
Horncastle
Spilsby
Skegness
Ingoldmills
Chapel St Leonards
Woodhall Spa
Tattershall
Coningsby
Wainfleet All Saints
Gibraltar Pt
Sleaford
BOSTON
Sibsey
Old Leake
Wrangle
Kirton
Swineshead
Donington
Gosberton
Surfleet
Spalding
Holbeach
Long Sutton
Sutton Bridge
Bourne
Market Deeping
Deeping St James
Crowland
Stamford
Wisbech
KING'S LYNN
Terrington St Clement
Downham Market
Outwell
Upwell
March
Chatteris
Whittlesey
PETERBOROUGH
Old Fletton
Oundle
Thrapston
Ramsey
Warboys
Somersham
Sawtry
Yaxley
Ely
Littleport
THE WASH
Boston Deeps
Lynn Deep
Long Sand
Roger Sand
Toft Sand
Gat Sand
Seal Sand
Peter Black Sand
Bulldog Sand
Danger Zone
Bedford Level
Middle Level
CAMBRIDGE
2
3
4
5
6
7
8
9
40
31
32
47

A
B
C
D
E
F
G
47
1
2
3
4
5
6
7
8
9
39
32
Skegness
Chapel St Leonards
Ingoldmells
Ingoldmells Point
Hogsthorpe
Willoughby
Alford
Spilsby
Old Bolingbroke
Horncastle
Burgh le Marsh
Wainfleet All Saints
Gibraltar Pt.
Stickney
Sibsey
Boston
Kirton
Wigtoft
Sutterton
Fosdyke
Holbeach
Moulton
Whaplode
Spalding
Long Sutton
Sutton Bridge
Gedney Drove End
Terrington St Clement
King's Lynn
Gaywood
West Lynn
Wisbech
Walsoken
Outwell
Upwell
Downham Market
Denver
Hilgay
Southery
Methwold
Feltwell
Brandon
Thetford
Thetford Forest
Swaffham
Narborough
Castle Acre
Fakenham
Wells-next-the-Sea
Holkham
Burnham Market
Hunstanton
Heacham
Sedgeford
Docking
Snettisham
Dersingham
Sandringham
Grimston
Gayton
Middleton
March
Chatteris
Ramsey
Whittlesey
Ely
Littleport
Lakenheath
Mundford
Weeting
Hockwold cum Wilton
The Wash
Boston Deep
Long Sand
Lynn Deep
Roger Sand
Toft Sand
Gat Sand
Seal Sand
Peter Black Sand
Bulldog Sand
Old South
Breast Sand
Danger Zone
Middle Level
Bedford Level
Marshland Fen
Breckland
Holme next the Sea
Titchwell
Brancaster
A16
A17
A52
A47
A10
A134
A1065
A149
A148
A1101
A141
A142

G
H
J
K
L
M
N
1
2
3
4
5
6
7
8
9
Blakeney Point
Peddars Way & Norfolk Coast Path
THE MUCKLEBURGH MILITARY COLLECTION
Sheringham
West Runton
Cromer
Overstrand
Sidestrand
Trimingham
Mundesley
Paston
Bacton
Keswick
Walcott
Happisburgh
Whimpwell Green
Hempstead
Sea Palling
Waxham
Horsey
Winterton-on-Sea
Hemsby
Newport
Scratby
California
Caister-on-Sea
GREAT YARMOUTH
Gorleston on Sea
Hopton
Corton
LOWESTOFT
Lowestoft Ness
Pakefield
Kessingland
Kessingland Beach
Covehithe
South Cove
Blackwater
North Walsham
Aylsham
Holt
East Dereham
Wymondham
Attleborough
Diss
Harleston
Bungay
Beccles
Halesworth
Hoveton
Horning
Acle
Reedham
Loddon
Brundall
Drayton
Costessey
Hethersett
NORWICH
THE BROADS
Stalham
Ludham
Fakenham
Reepham
Hingham
Long Stratton
Pulham Market
Thetford
Oulton Broad
Worlingham
Wrentham
Blythburgh
Southwold
Barsham
NORFOLK
33

A
B
C
48
D
E
F
G
1
2
3
4
5
6
7
8
9
35
ISLE OF MAN
Point of Ayre
The Ayres
Rue Point
Jurby Head
Sartfield
Ballasalla
Crawyn
The Cronk
Orrisdale
Orrisdale Head
Kirk Michael
Ballacarnane Beg
Barregarrow
Shoughlaige-e-Caine
Gob y Deigan
Knocksharry
St Patrick's Isle
Peel
Contrary Head
Knockaloe Moar
Patrick
Glenmaye
Dalby Point
Niarbyl Island
Niarbyl Bay
Dalby
Dalby Mountain
South Barrule
Stroin Vuigh
Lingague
Fleshwick Bay
Bradda East
Bradda Head
Port Erin
Calf of Man
Chicken Rock
Spanish Head
Port St Mary
Castletown
Langness
Dreswick Point
Derbyhaven
St Michael's Island
Ballasalla
Santon Head
Little Ness
Douglas Head
DOUGLAS
Douglas Bay
Onchan
Onchan Head
Port Groudle
Clay Head
Garwick Bay
Baldrine
Laxey
Laxey Head
Laxey Bay
Bulgham Bay
Dhoon
Port Cornaa
Port Mooar
Maughold
Maughold Head
Ramsey
RAMSEY BAY
Shellag Point
Bride
Cranstal
Andreas
Jurby
Sulby
St Judes
Ballaugh
Ravensdale
Churchtown
Glen Auldyn
Snaefell
Sulby Resr
Little London
Cronk-y-Voddy
Lambfell Moar
Injebreck
Baldwin
Greeba Mountain
Crosby
Foxdale
Glen Vine
Union Mills
Strang
Braddan
Stuggadhoo
Newtown
Ballamodha
Ballabeg
Colby
Ballafesson
Cregneish
Ballakilpheric
Ronague
Grenaby
Belfast (summer only)
Ardrossan (summer weekends only)
Heysham
Fleetwood (summer only)
Liverpool
Dublin (summer only)
Douglas, Isle of Man
Douglas, Isle of Man (summer only)
Silecroft
Kirksanton
Millom
Haverigg
Haverigg Point
Duddon Sands
Askam in Furness
Ulverston
Dalton-in-Furness
BARROW-IN-FURNESS
North Scale
Vickerstown
Tummer Hill Scar
Biggar
ISLE OF WALNEY
South End
Roa Island
Rampside
Foulney Island
Piel Island
Hilpsford Point
Bardsea
Baycliff
Aldingham
Newbiggin
Mort Bank
Rossall Point
FLEETWOOD
Cleveleys
Little Bispham
Norbreck
Bispham
North Shore
Poulton-le-Fylde
BLACKPOOL
BLACKPOOL TOWER
South Shore
PLEASURE BEACH
Squires Gate
LYTHAM ST ANNE'S
Salter's Bank
Horse Bank
Angry Brow
SOUTHPORT
PLEASURELAND
Ainsdale
Formby Point
Formby
Danger Zone
Hightown
Little Crosby
CROSBY
Great Crosby
Waterloo
Seaforth
Crosby Channel
Belfast
LIVERPOOL BAY
BOOTLE
WALLASEY
New Brighton
East Hoyle Bank
Hoylake
West Hoyle Bank
Hilbre Island
BIRKENHEAD
Moreton

G
H
J
K
49
L
M
N
YORKSHIRE
DALES
NORTH
NATIONAL
PARK
LANCASHIRE
GREATER
MANCHESTER
MORECAMBE
HEYSHAM
LANCASTER
Carnforth
Grange-over-Sands
Arnside
Silverdale
Kirkby Lonsdale
Burton-in-Kendal
Ingleton
Settle
Skipton
Clitheroe
Barnoldswick
Earby
Colne
NELSON
Brierfield
BURNLEY
Padiham
Great Harwood
Clayton-le-Moors
Rishton
Church
ACCRINGTON
Oswaldtwistle
BLACKBURN
DARWEN
Longridge
PRESTON
Fulwood
Kirkham
Leyland
CHORLEY
Haslingden
RAWTENSTALL
Bacup
Todmorden
Hebden Bridge
Ramsbottom
BURY
ROCHDALE
HEYWOOD
Littleborough
Milnrow
Royton
OLDHAM
MIDDLETON
CHADDERTON
RADCLIFFE
Whitefield
Prestwich
FARNWORTH
BOLTON
Horwich
Adlington
Standish
WIGAN
Orrell
Ashton-in-Makerfield
Hindley
Westhoughton
ATHERTON
Tyldesley
LEIGH
WORSLEY
Swinton
Pendlebury
SALFORD
MANCHESTER
ECCLES
STRETFORD
URMSTON
SALE
ALTRINCHAM
ASHTON-UNDER-LYNE
STALYBRIDGE
Dukinfield
Droylsden
FAILSWORTH
DENTON
HYDE
STOCKPORT
CHEADLE
Marple
ST. HELENS
NEWTON-LE-WILLOWS
WARRINGTON
Haydock
Golborne
KIRKBY
Prescot
Huyton
Rainford
SKELMERSDALE
ORMSKIRK
Burscough
44
1
2
3
4
5
6
7
8
9
45
43

A
B
C
D
E
F
G
1
2
3
4
5
6
7
8
9
43
42
36
L A N C A S H I R E
G R E A T E R
M A N C H E S T E R
S E Y S I D E
Carnforth
Bolton-le-Sands
Hest Bank
Morecambe
Heysham
Lancaster
Galgate
Forest of Bowland
Settle
Long Preston
Hellifield
Gargrave
Skipton
Clitheroe
Barnoldswick
Earby
Colne
Nelson
Burnley
Padiham
Accrington
Great Harwood
Oswaldtwistle
Blackburn
Darwen
Preston
Fulwood
Longridge
Kirkham
Freckleton
Leyland
Chorley
Garstang
Haslingden
Rawtenstall
Bacup
Todmorden
Hebden Bridge
Ramsbottom
Edgworth
Rochdale
Heywood
Bury
Bolton
Horwich
Adlington
Standish
Wigan
Ormskirk
Skelmersdale
Kirkby
Atherton
Leigh
Farnworth
Radcliffe
Whitefield
Middleton
Chadderton
Oldham
Prestwich
Failsworth
Ashton-under-Lyne
Stalybridge
Dukinfield
Droylsden
Manchester
Salford
Eccles
Swinton
Stretford
Urmston
Sale
Altrincham
Denton
Hyde
Stockport
Cheadle
Gatley
Bramhall
Hazel Grove
Marple
Wilmslow
Knutsford
Warrington
Widnes
Runcorn
Ellesmere Port
Liverpool
Huyton
Prescot
St Helens
Haydock
Newton-le-Willows
Golborne
Ashton-in-Makerfield
Hindley
Westhoughton
Tyldesley
Lymm
Irlam
Ripponden
Littleborough
Whitworth
Wardle
Milnrow
Royton
Shaw
Mossley
Bredbury
Romiley
Bollington
Poynton
Whaley Bridge
Trawden
The Forest of Trawden
Brierfield
Bentham
High Bentham
Ingleton
Whalley
Billington
Wilpshire
Rishton
Clayton-le-Moors
Walton-le-Dale
Bamber Bridge
Lostock Hall
Penwortham
Hutton
Tarleton
Much Hoole
Hesketh Bank
Rufford
Croston
Burscough
Coppull
Tottington
Egerton
Belmont
Rivington
Little Lever
Walkden
Worsley
Partington
Hale
Bowdon
Timperley
Poulton
Tatham
Wray
Hornby
Halton
Caton
Glasson
Cockerham
Pilling
Preesall
Stalmine
Hambleton
Out Rawcliffe
St Michael's on Wyre
Catterall
Bilsborrow
Broughton
Goosnargh
Chipping
Dunsop Bridge
Newton
Slaidburn
Gisburn
Sawley
Chatburn
Downham
Rimington
Waddington
Grindleton
Bolton by Bowland
Pendle Hill
The Forest of Pendle
Barrowford
Foulridge
Kelbrook
Salterforth
Thornton-in-Craven
Elslack
Carleton
Embsay
Cononley
Sutton-in-Craven
Cowling
Silsden
Kildwick
Glusburn
Steeton
Keighley
Oxenhope
Haworth
Oakworth
Stanbury
Laneshawbridge
Wycoller
Worsthorne
Cliviger
Holme Chapel
Cornholme
Walsden
Mytholmroyd
Sowerby Bridge
Heptonstall
Rochdale
Norden
Shawclough
Whitworth
Smallbridge
Denshaw
Delph
Greenfield
Uppermill
Diggle
Castleshaw Moss
Springhead
Lees
Grasscroft
Tintwistle
Hollingworth
Mottram in Longdendale
Hattersley
Gee Cross
Woodley
Compstall
Hadfield
Charlesworth
Chisworth
Mellor
Disley
New Mills
Furness Vale
Kettleshulme
Adlington
Prestbury
Handforth
Styal
Mobberley
Ashley
Rostherne
High Legh
Appleton
Stockton Heath
Grappenhall
Thelwall
Culcheth
Glazebury
Croft
Winwick
Burtonwood
Penketh
Great Sankey
Cronton
Halewood
Hale
Speke
Garston
Allerton
Woolton
Childwall
Knotty Ash
Roby
Whiston
Rainhill
Rainford
Billinge
Orrell
Up Holland
Parbold
Appley Bridge
Shevington
Newburgh
Dalton
Aughton
Maghull
Lydiate
Melling
Bickerstaffe
Hesketh Lane
Ribchester
Salesbury
Mellor
Balderstone
Samlesbury
Higher Walton
Hoghton
Brindle
Withnell
Wheelton
Whittle-le-Woods
Clayton-le-Woods
Euxton
Eccleston
Mawdesley
Wrightington
Heskin
Charnock Richard
Clifton
Salwick
Elswick
Great Eccleston
Inskip
Woodplumpton
Barton
Wrea Green
Warton
Lytham St Annes
Ribble

G
H
J
K
L
M
N
50
37
46
2
3
4
5
6
7
8
9
HARROGATE
Knaresborough
Ripon
Boroughbridge
YORK
Y O R K
Selby
ILKLEY
Otley
Wetherby
Tadcaster
Garforth
Castleford
Pontefract
LEEDS
BRADFORD
HALIFAX
HUDDERSFIELD
BRIGHOUSE
DEWSBURY
WAKEFIELD
MORLEY
PUDSEY
BATLEY
ROTHWELL
Ossett
Mirfield
Elland
SHIPLEY
BINGLEY
Keighley
Baildon
Guiseley
Yeadon
Holmfirth
Meltham
Penistone
BARNSLEY
Darfield
Wombwell
Hoyland
Stocksbridge
Mexborough
Conisbrough
DONCASTER
BENTLEY
ROTHERHAM
SHEFFIELD
Maltby
Tickhill
Dinnington
WORKSOP
RETFORD
EAST RETFORD
Goole
Thorne
Snaith
Hemsworth
Cudworth
Royston
Featherstone
Normanton
Knottingley
Sherburn in Elmet
Tockwith
Bramham
Clifford
Boston Spa
Easingwold
Stillington
Pocklington
Thurnscoe
Goldthorpe
Adwick le Street
Swinton
Rawmarsh
Wath upon Dearne
Kiveton Park
Dronfield
Chesterfield
Harworth
Bawtry
Finningley
Hatfield
Pateley Bridge
W E S T
Y O R K S H I R E
S O U T H
P E A K

A
B
C
D
E
F
G
50
1
2
3
4
5
6
7
8
9
YORK
EAST
OF
LINCOL
SOUTH
YORKSHIRE
Knaresborough
HARROGATE
Wetherby
Tadcaster
GARFORTH
ROTHWELL
MORLEY
DEWSBURY
WAKEFIELD
Normanton
CASTLEFORD
PONTEFRACT
Knottingley
Featherstone
Hemsworth
BARNSLEY
Wombwell
Mexborough
Swinton
Conisbrough
ROTHERHAM
SHEFFIELD
Dronfield
Staveley
CHESTERFIELD
Bolsover
WORKSOP
Market Warsop
RETFORD (EAST RETFORD)
Gainsborough
Bawtry
Tickhill
Maltby
DONCASTER
BENTLEY
Adwick le Street
Thorne
Hatfield
Selby
Goole
Rawcliffe
Snaith
Howden
Pocklington
Market Weighton
Stamford Bridge
Tollerton
Shipton
Strensall
Haxby
Crockey Hill
Sherburn in Elmet
Thurnscoe
Goldthorpe
Darfield
Hoyland
Penistone
Stocksbridge
Chapeltown
Ecclesfield
Kiveton Park
Dinnington
Crowle
Epworth
SCUNTHORPE
Ashby
Bottesford
Kirton in Lindsey
Blyton
Misterton
North Wheatley
Sturton le Steeple
Tuxford
Saxilby
Skellingthorpe
Clowne
Killamarsh
Eckington
Beighton
Harworth
Blyth
Carlton in Lindrick
Thorpe Willoughby
Brayton
Drax
Airmyn
Hook
Saltmarshe
Whitgift
Adlingfleet
Burton upon Stather
Alkborough
Winteringham
Whitton
Barmby Moor
Holme-on-Spalding-Moor
North Cave
Newport
Gilberdyke
Staddlethorpe
M1
M18
M62
M180
M181
M621
A1(M)
38
45

G
H
J
K
L
M
N
BAY
1
2
3
4
5
6
7
8
9
Great Driffield
Hornsea
BEVERLEY
Cottingham
CITY OF KINGSTON UPON HULL
KINGSTON UPON HULL
Hessle
Hedon
Withernsea
Barton-upon-Humber
Immingham
HUMBER
MOUTH OF THE HUMBER
Spurn Head
GRIMSBY
CLEETHORPES
Rotterdam & Zeebrugge
N.E. LINCOLNSHIRE
Brigg
Market Rasen
Louth
Mablethorpe
Sutton on Sea
Alford
Chapel St Leonards
Ingoldmells
Danger Zone
Danger Area
RIDING
YORKSHIRE
LINCOLNSHIRE

A
B
C
D
E
F
G
53
42
Castle Douglas
Dalbeattie
Kirkcudbright
Annan
Bowness-on-Solway
Silloth
Wigton
Maryport
WORKINGTON
Cockermouth
WHITEHAVEN
Keswick
St Bees
Egremont
Seascale
Ravenglass
Millom
Ulverston
Aspatria
Allonby
Abbeytown
Kirkbean
Southerness
Mersehead Sands
Preston Merse
Barnhourie Sands
Blackshaw Bank
SOLWAY FIRTH
St Bees Head
WHINLATTER FOREST PARK
LAKE
NATIONAL
Danger Zone
Haverigg
Broughton in Furness
Coniston
Grasmere
Threlkeld
Gretna
New Abbey
Ruthwell
Cummertrees
Dundrennan
Auchencairn
Rockcliffe
Kippford
Palnackie
Bootle
Gosforth
Cleator Moor
Frizington
Distington
Harrington
Flimby
Dearham
Crosscanonby
Skinburness
Kirkbride
Dalston
Caldbeck
Ireby
Wasdale Head
Eskdale Green
Boot
Holmrook
Drigg
Sellafield
Calder Bridge
Ennerdale Bridge
Loweswater
Buttermere
Seatoller
Rosthwaite
Braithwaite
Thornthwaite
Bassenthwaite
Low Lorton
High Lorton

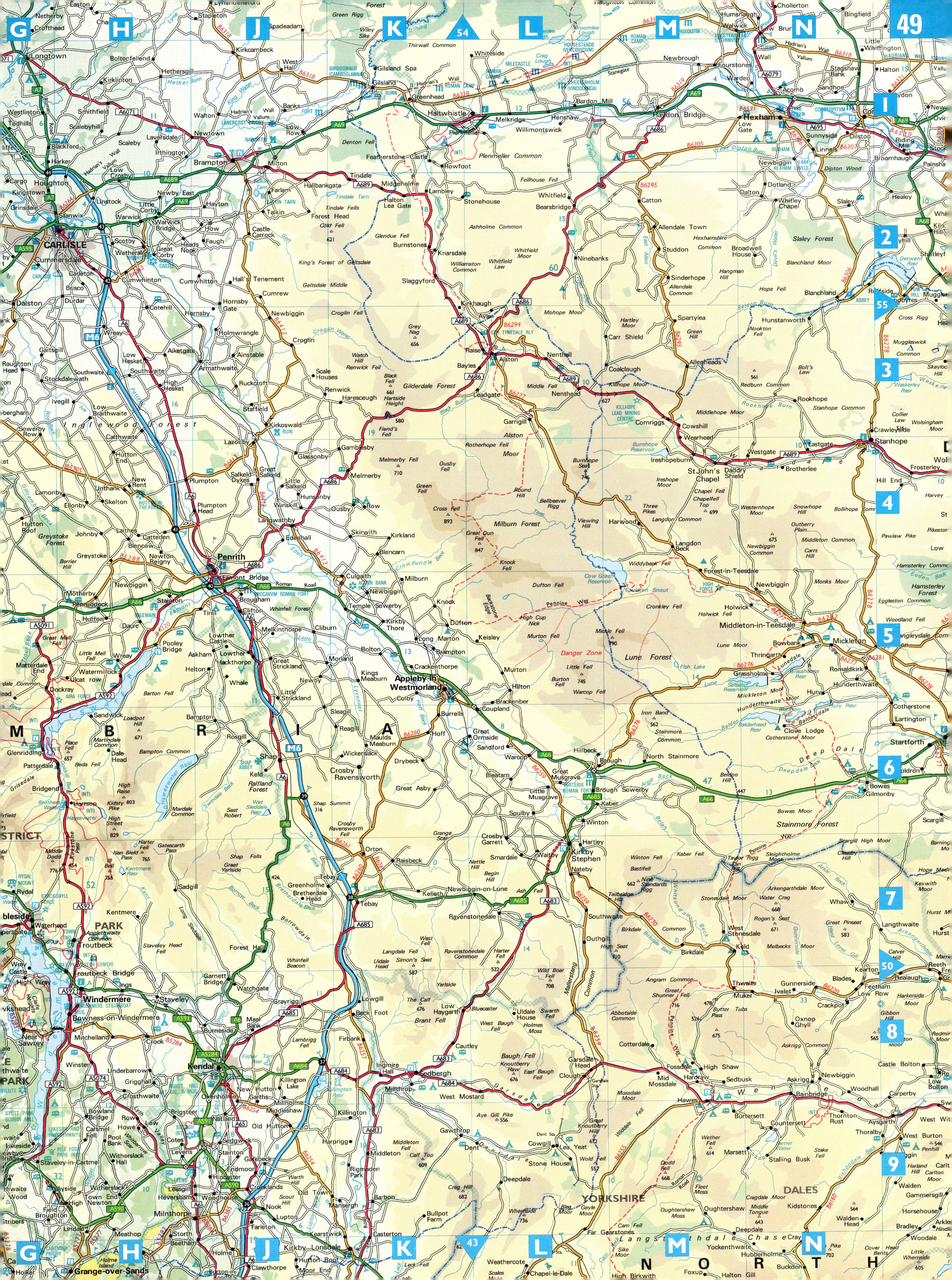
G
H
J
K
54
L
M
N
CARLISLE
Longtown
Brampton
Haltwhistle
Greenhead
Gilsland Spa
Bardon Mill
Haydon Bridge
Hexham
Corbridge
Penrith
Appleby-in-Westmorland
Alston
Nenthead
Garrigill
Stanhope
St John's Chapel
Middleton-in-Teesdale
Mickleton
Romaldkirk
Cotherstone
Startforth
Bowes
Brough
Kirkby Stephen
Tebay
Orton
Shap
Ravenstonedale
Kendal
Windermere
Bowness-on-Windermere
Staveley
Sedbergh
Dent
Hawes
Askrigg
Bainbridge
Carperby
Milnthorpe
Kirkby Lonsdale
Grange-over-Sands
Ambleside
Troutbeck
Pooley Bridge
Lazonby
Kirkoswald
Melmerby
Allendale Town
Allenheads
Cross Fell
893
Milburn Forest
Lune Forest
Stainmore Forest
Inglewood Forest
Ashholme Common
Cow Green Reservoir
Danger Zone
YORKSHIRE
DALES
Langstrothdale Chase
NORTH
M6
A6
A66
A69
A686
A689
A685
A683
A684
A591
A590
A65
43
1
2
3
4
5
6
7
8
9
50
55

A
B
C
D
E
F
G
1
2
3
4
5
6
7
8
9
55
49
45
46
CONSETT
DURHAM
D U R H A M
Stanhope
Wolsingham
Crook
Willington
Spennymoor
BISHOP AUCKLAND
Shildon
Newton Aycliffe
DARLINGTON
HARTLEPOOL
H A R T L E P O O L
MIDDLESBROUGH
STOCKTON ON TEES
REDCAR AND CLEVELAND
Guisborough
Barnard Castle
Richmond
Northallerton
Thirsk
Ripon
Bedale
Leyburn
Middleham
Masham
Pateley Bridge
Grassington
Boroughbridge
Knaresborough
Catterick Camp
Yarm
Stokesley
Great Ayton
Peterlee
Seaham
Sedgefield
Houghton le Spring
Easingwold
T H Y O R K S H I R E
NORTH
Danger Zone
A1(M)
A66(M)

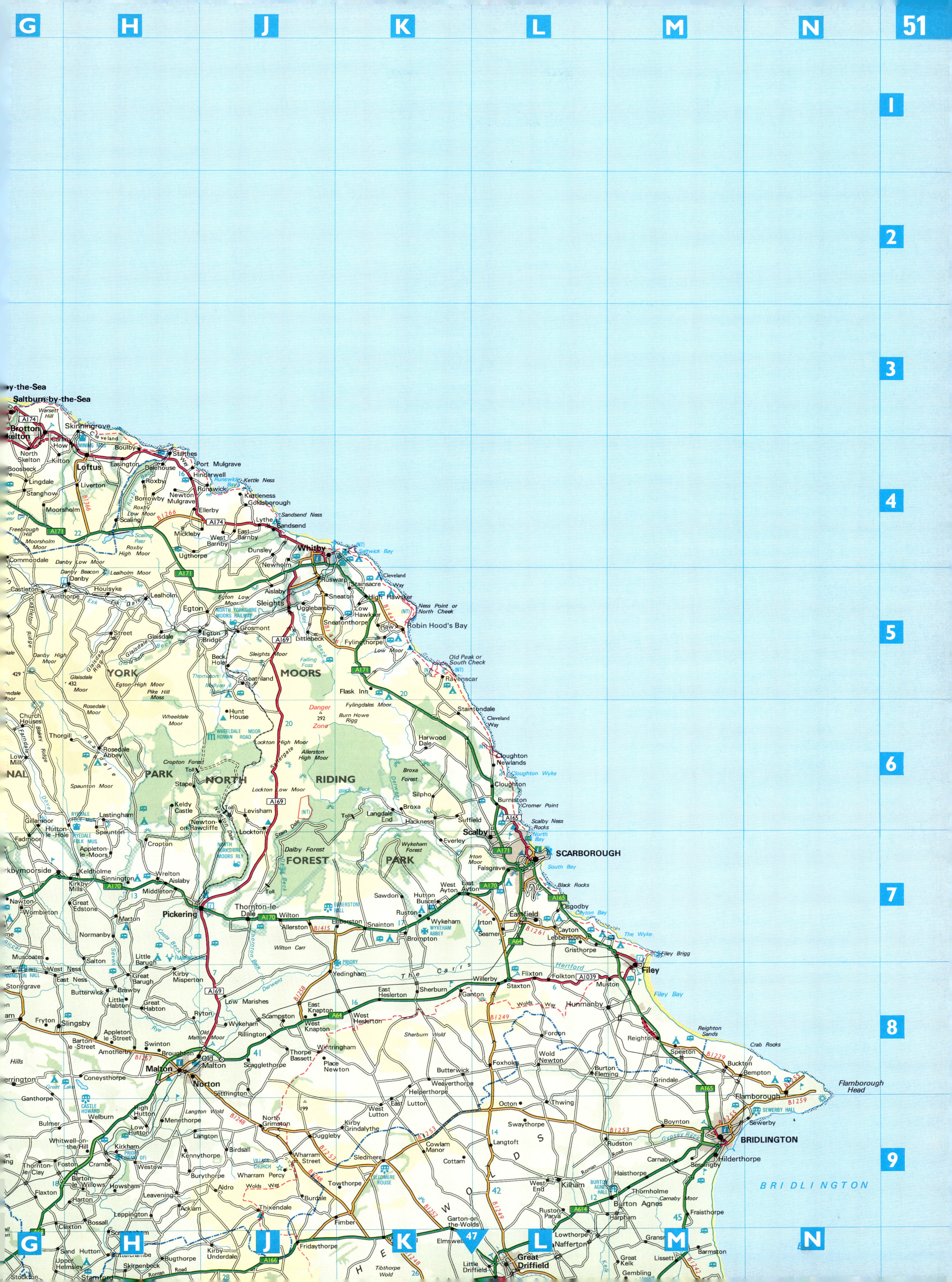
G
H
J
K
L
M
N
1
2
3
4
5
6
7
8
9
Saltburn-by-the-Sea
Brotton
Skinningrove
Loftus
Staithes
Port Mulgrave
Hinderwell
Runswick
Kettleness
Goldsborough
Sandsend Ness
Lythe
Sandsend
Whitby
Saltwick Bay
Ruswarp
Stainsacre
Hawsker
Sneaton
Sleights
Egton
Grosmont
Robin Hood's Bay
Ness Point or North Cheek
Fylingthorpe
Old Peak or South Cheek
Ravenscar
Goathland
YORK
MOORS
NORTH
RIDING
PARK
FOREST
Danby
Castleton
Lealholm
Glaisdale
Rosedale Abbey
Lastingham
Hutton-le-Hole
Kirkbymoorside
Pickering
Levisham
Lockton
Flask Inn
Fylingdales Moor
Staintondale
Harwood Dale
Cloughton
Cloughton Wyke
Burniston
Scalby
Scalby Ness
SCARBOROUGH
South Bay
Cayton Bay
Osgodby
Cayton
Filey Brigg
Filey
Filey Bay
Hunmanby
Reighton
Speeton
Bempton
Buckton
Flamborough
Flamborough Head
SEWERBY HALL
Sewerby
BRIDLINGTON
Hilderthorpe
BRIDLINGTON BAY
Malton
Norton
Old Malton
Slingsby
CASTLE HOWARD
Rillington
Scampston
Sherburn
Ganton
Staxton
Seamer
Eastfield
Thornton-le-Dale
Wykeham
Ebberston
Snainton
Brompton
Yedingham
East Heslerton
West Heslerton
Wintringham
Settrington
North Grimston
Wharram le Street
Duggleby
Sledmere
Kirby Grindalythe
Cowlam Manor
Langtoft
Foxholes
Wold Newton
Burton Fleming
Thwing
Rudston
Boynton
Carnaby
Kilham
Burton Agnes
Great Driffield
Nafferton
Garton-on-the-Wolds
Fridaythorpe
Thixendale
Birdsall
Langton
Westow
Kirkham
Whitwell-on-the-Hill
Flaxton
Stamford Bridge
Great Kelk
Barmston
Fraisthorpe

A
B
C
58
D
E
F
G
1
2
3
4
5
6
7
8
9
Shannochie
Bennan Head
Sound of Pladda
Pladda
Levencorroch
Dippin
Dippin Head
Heads of Ayr
AYR
Belston
Sundrum
Trabboch
Ochiltree
Holmston
Joppa
Coylton
Seafield
Alloway
Drongan
Burnton
Sinclairston
Lagg
Fisherton
Dunure
Brown Carrick Hill
Nether Auchendrane
Mount Oliphant
Hollybush
Littlemill
Dunure Mains
Sauchrie
Culroy
Dalrymple
Rankinston
Knoweside
Minishant
Skeldon
Culzean Bay
Grimmet
Dalvennan
Patna
Lethanhill
Maybole
Kirkmichael
Waterside
Benbeoch
Maidens
Morriston
Kirkoswald
Crossraguel Abbey
Turnberry Bay
Turnberry
Crosshill
Blairquhan
Burnton
Dalmellington
Clawfin
Gass
Straiton
Craigoch
Dalcairnie
Craigengillan
SOUTH
AYRSHIRE
Kilkerran
Dipple
Dowhill
Wallacetown
Craig
Maraiz Hill
Low Craighead
Dailly
Bargany
Tairlaw
Eriff
Chapeldonan
Grangeston
Old Dailly
Pinkill
Hadyard Hill
Garleffin Fell
429
Ailsa Craig
Girvan
Saugh Hill
Penwhapple Reservoir
Linfern Loch
Loch Bradan Reservoir
Loch Doon
Glendoune
Glengennet
North Balloch
Lamloch
Black Neuk
Glendrissaig
South Balloch
Waterhead
Craiglee
Brochloch
Ardwell
Kennedy's Pass
Pinminnoch
Changue Forest
Nick of the Balloch Pass
Shiel Hill
Starr
Grey Hill
297
Barr
341
Shalloch
Loch Head
C A R R I C K
565
Polmaddie Hill
Shalloch on Minnoch
Lendalfoot
Pinmore
479
Carleton Fishery
Aldons
GALLOWAY
Daljarrock
Poundland
Pinwherry
Bennane Head
Colmonell
Dalreoch
Glenduisk
FOREST
Ballantrae Bay
Knockdolian
Craigneil
Black Clauchrie
PARK
Mains of Tig
Ballochmorrie
Garwall Hill
Palgowan
Ballantrae
Barrhill
Auchairne
Balkissock
Shiel Hill
Eldrick
Glen Trool Lodge
Downan Point
Glenapp Castle
Smyrton
Lochton
Corwar House
Glentrool
Craigencallie
Beneraird
439
Craigie Fell
Carlock Hill
Milljoan Hill
Drumlamford Loch
Drumlamford Ho
Mulldonoch
Lamachan Hill
716
Chirmorrie
Bargrennan
Altimeg Hill
Larg Hill
Millfore
Finnarts Point
Larne
Belfast
Milleur Point
Glen App
Markdhu
Clachaneasy
Larg
Corsewall Point
Barnhills
Miltonise
Polbae
Garlick Hill
North Cairn
Glenwhilly
Knockville
Dalnigap
Kirkcolm
Corsewall
Cairnryan
Urrall Fell
Garlies Castle
South Cairn
Cairn Point
Dounan Bay
Airies
Ervie
Artfield Fell
Renninghame
Boreland
Cumloden
Carseriggan
Glenrazie
Minnigaff
Portobello
St Mary's Croft
Braid Fell
Challoch
Soleburn Bridge
Balminnoch
Newton Stewart
Blackcraig
Knocknain
Leswalt
Culvennan Fell
Palnure
Slouchnawen Bay
New Luce
Tarf Bridge
Shennanton
Nether Barr
Bennfield
Cairnsmore
Innermessan
Auchmantle
Lochinch Castle
Galdenoch
Baltersan
Stranraer
Castle Kennedy
Craig Fell
Carscreugh
Barlae
Craighlaw
Kirkcowan
Spittal
Broadsea Bay
Portslogan
Causeway End
Creetown
Dunragit Moor
Whitecairn
Carsegowan
Black Head
Whiteleys
Dunragit
Glenluce
Knock Moss
Spittal
Cassencarie
Lochans
Kildrochet
Genoch
Culquhirk
Wigtown Sands
Cairn Pat
Genoch Square
Knock Fell
Carsluith
Dinvin
Colfin
Sands of Luce
Bladnoch
Wigtown
Portpatrick
Awhirk
Crow's Nest
Corsemalzie
Baldoon Sands
Kirkdale
Stoneykirk
Auchenmalg
Port of Spittal Bay
Barnbarroch
Kirkinner
Balgreggan
Culshabbin
Sandhead
Cairngarroch Bay
Whauphill
Stewarton
Money Head
Alticry
Loch Head
Eggerness
Elrig
Clachanmore
Kirkland of Longcastle
Sorbie
Garlieston
L U C E   B A Y
Ardwell
Mochrum
Airyhassen
Ardwell Bay
Chapel Rossan
T H E   M A C H A R S
Barr Point
Cruggleton Bay
Logan
Port William
Barwinnock
Drumbreddan Bay
Balgowan
Danger Zone
Cults
Mull of Logan
Castlewigg
Port Logan
Terally
Barsalloch Point
Monreith
Port Allen
Monreith Bay
Craigdhu
Whithorn
Kilstay
Cairndoon
Glasserton
Portyerrock
Clanyard Bay
Fell of Carleton
Kirkmaiden
Drummore
Kidsdale
Laggantalluch Head
Damnaglaur
Cailiness Point
St Ninian's Cave
Port Castle Bay
Isle of Whithorn
Maryport
Cutcloy
Crammag Head
Dunman
Scares
Devil's Bridge
Nick of Kindram
Burrow Head
Portankill
East Tarbert
West Tarbert
Mull of Galloway
A77
A75
A714
A747
A716
A718
A751
A746
A712
A713
A719
A70
B734
B741
B7023
B7024
B7084
B7077
B7042
B7005
B7052
B7004
B7021
B7044
B7043
B738
B798
B733
B7027

G
H
J
K
L
M
N
59
54
48
1
2
3
4
5
6
7
8
9
DUMFRIES
AND
GALLOWAY
SOLWAY
FIRTH
Cumnock
New Cumnock
Kirkconnel
Sanquhar
Leadhills
Wanlockhead
Crawford
Moffat
Thornhill
Penpont
Moniaive
Lochmaben
Lockerbie
Ecclefechan
Annan
Dumfries
New Abbey
Dalbeattie
Castle Douglas
New Galloway
St John's Town of Dalry
Gatehouse of Fleet
Kirkcudbright
Silloth
Maryport
Workington
Cockermouth
Aspatria
Allonby
Wigton
Kirkbride
Bowness-on-Solway
Blackshaw Bank
Mersehead Sands
Barnhourie Sands
Southerness Point
Abbey Head
Little Ross
Danger Zone
Forest of Ae
Dalveen Pass
Lowther Hills
Beattock Summit
Devil's Beef Tub
Tweed's Well
Carsethorn
Kippford or Scaur
Rockcliffe
Auchencairn
Kirkpatrick Durham
Crocketford or Ninemile Bar
Springholm
Haugh of Urr
Palnackie
Gelston
Twynholm
Borgue
Kirkandrews
Dundrennan
Powfoot
Ruthwell
Clarencefield
Carrutherstown
Collin
Torthorwald
Tinwald
Amisfield Town
Templand
Johnstonebridge
Beattock
Closeburn
Durisdeer
Kirkland
Dunscore
Holywood
Auldgirth
Kirkbean
Caulkerbush
Mainsriddle
Southerness
Balmae
Ross
Dubmill Point
Beckfoot
Abbeytown
Newton Arlosh
Flimby
Dearham
Great Broughton
Brigham
Crosby
Ellenborough
WHINLATTER FOREST PARK
A74(M)
A76
A75
A701
A702
A710
A711
A712
A713
A762
A709
A596
A595
A66
A591
B5300
B729
B7020
B724
B725

A
B
C
D
E
F
G
1
2
3
4
5
6
7
8
9
60
53
49
Langholm
Canonbie
Longtown
CARLISLE
Brampton
Haltwhistle
Penrith
Keswick
Appleby-in-Westmorland
Wigton
Annan
Gretna
Lockerbie
Newcastleton
Kielder
KIELDER FOREST PARK
NORTHUMBERLAND NATIONAL PARK
Kershope Forest
Castle O'er Forest
Inglewood Forest
Bowness-on-Solway
Dalston
Aspatria
Caldbeck
Sebergham
Alston
Greenhead
Bellingham
Falstone
Gilsland
Hexham
Kirkoswald
Lazonby
Temple Sowerby
Threlkeld
WHINLATTER FOREST PARK
Skiddaw Forest
Gilderdale Forest
Milburn Forest
Kirkbride
Burgh by Sands
Rockcliffe
Stanwix
Houghton
Scaleby
Irthington
Castle Carrock
Cumwhitton
Armathwaite
Hesket Newmarket
Greystoke
Eamont Bridge
Stainton
Ecclefechan
Kirkpatrick-Fleming
Middlebie
Eskdalemuir
Bentpath
Kirkstile
Teviothead
Hawick
Hermitage
Saughtree
Byrness
Catcleugh
Otterburn
Southdean
Chesters
Bonchester Bridge
Hobkirk
Wolfelee
Glenkerry
Craik Forest
Deanburnhaugh
Broadhaugh
Northhouse
Branxholme
Black Knowe
Shankend
Greenhaugh
Stannersburn
Lanehead
Charlton
Hesleyside
Bower
Tarset
Wark Forest
Spadeadam Forest
Bewcastle
Roadhead
Kirkcambeck
Lanercost
Hadrian's Wall
Cross Fell
Dufton
Murton
Knock
Long Marton
Kirkby Thore
Culgaith
Langwathby
Great Salkeld
Plumpton
Skelton
Hutton Roof
Mungrisdale
Blencathra
Saddleback
M6
A7
A74(M)
A69
A686
A595
A596
A66
A6
A68
A6071
A689
A6088
A591
A5091
A592

G
H
J
K
L
M
N
61
50
1
2
3
4
5
6
7
8
9
NORTHUMBERLAND
DURHAM
TYNE & WEAR
HARTLEPOOL
STOCKTON ON TEES
Alnmouth
Amble
Coquet Island
Rothbury
Otterburn
Morpeth
ASHINGTON
Newbiggin-by-the-Sea
Bedlington
BLYTH
Seaton Delaval
WHITLEY BAY
TYNEMOUTH
SOUTH SHIELDS
NEWCASTLE UPON TYNE
GATESHEAD
WHICKHAM
Wallsend
Jarrow
Hebburn
FELLING
BOLDON
SUNDERLAND
Washington
Chester-le-Street
STANLEY
CONSETT
Hexham
Corbridge
Prudhoe
Ponteland
Blaydon
Ryton
HOUGHTON LE SPRING
Hetton-le-Hole
SEAHAM
Peterlee
DURHAM
Spennymoor
Crook
Willington
BISHOP AUCKLAND
Shildon
Newton Aycliffe
Sedgefield
Billingham
MIDDLESBROUGH
Barnard Castle
Middleton-in-Teesdale
Stanhope
Wolsingham
Harwood Forest
Hamburg (summer only)
Stavanger, Haugesund & Bergen
Göteborg (summer only)
Ijmuiden
A1
A68
A69
A696
A697
A1(M)
A194(M)
A167(M)
A19
A689
A690
A692
A693

A
B
C
62
D
E
F
G
1
2
3
4
5
6
7
8
9
Port Lotha
Garvard
Balerominmore
Balerominduhb
Sguide Loinne
Rubha Ban
Oronsay
Dubh Eilean
Eilean nan Ron
Eilean Ghaoideamal
Caolas Mor
Sgeir Mhor a'Bhrein-phuirt
Rubh' an t-Sailein
Rubh' a'Chrois-aoinidh
Rubh' a'Mhail
Rubha Bholsa
Sgarbh Breac
364
Margadale Hill
Nave Island
Ardnave Point
Gortantaoid Point
Ardnave
Killinallan Point
Killinallan
Tayovullin
Kilnave
Ton Mhor
Sanaigmore
Beinn Bhreac
286
Giur-bheinn
316
Bunnahabhainn
Ardnahoe
Balulive
Port Askaig
Keills
Feolin Ferry
Eilean Mor
Bralgo
Smaull
Leckgruinart
Rubha Lamanais
Ballinaby
Carnduncan
Aoradh
Gruinart
Craigens
Gruinart Flats
Ballygrant
Grainel
I
S
L
A
Y
Coul Point
Machir
Aruadh
Foreland
Lyrabus
Moin'a'choire
Esknish
Redhouses
Rockside
Kilchoman
Machir Bay
Conisby
Bruichladdich
Blackrock
A847
Islay Ho.
Bridgend
Cachlaidh Mhor
Neriby
Barr
Cattadale
Sgorr nam Faoileann
Beinn na Caillich
Glas Bheinn
471
McArthur's Head
Kilchiaran
Kilchiaran Bay
Bowmore
Gartnatra
Cruach
Cluanach
Gearach
Port Charlotte
Islay
Rhinns of
Gartbreck
Ronnachmore
Tormisdale
Beinn Tart a'Mhill
232
Lossit
Laggan
Proaig
Lossit Bay
Nerabolls
Beinn Bhan
Beinn Bheigeir
491
Ardtalla
Rubha Liath
Easter Ellister
Portnahaven
Port Wemyss
Orsay
Rinns Point
Laggan Bay
Beinn Uraraidh
454
Loch Uraraidh
Claggain Bay
Trudernish
Kintour
Glenegedale
Islay (Port Ellen)
Sgorr Bhogachain
Ardmore Point
Ardmore
Beinn Sholum
347
Leorin
Leorin Lochs
Machrie
Eilean a'Chuirn
Eilean Bhride
Rubha Mor
Kintra
Cornabus
Ardbeg
Lagavulin
Laphroaig
Rubha na Gainmhich
Maol Buidhe
165
Carnmore
Port Ellen
The Ard
Texa
The Oa
Risabus
Lower Killeyan
Mull Of Oa
Loch Kinnabus
Inerval
Port Chubaird
Rubha nan Leacan
A846
B8016
B8017
B8018
Loch Indaal
Loch Gruinart
Sound of Islay
J
U
R
A
Dubh Bheinn
Beinn Bhreac
467
Rainberg Mor
453
Cruach Sgadail
Ardlussa
Inverlussa
Lussagiven
Lussa Point
Eilean an Rubha
Shian Bay
Loch Righ Mor
Gleann Aoistail
Beinn Sgillinish
Tarbert
Tarbert Bay
Loch Tarbert
Creag Nam Fiadh Mor
Glenbatrick
Scrinadle
Beinn Bhreac
439
Lagg
Gatehouse
Rubh' a'Chamais
Jura Forest
Beinn Tarsuinn
Achamore
Beinn an Oir
785
Beinn Shiantaidh
755
Paps of Jura
Ardmenish
Loch an t-Siob
Corran
An Dunan
Rubh 'an Leim
Beinn a'Chaolais
734
Knockrome
Lowlandman's Bay
Gleann Asdale
Leargybreck
Sron Garbh
Rubh 'an Leanachais
Glas Bheinn
561
Feolin
Eilean Bhride
Keils
Small Isles
Dubh Bheinn
Craighouse
Eilean nan Gabhar
Brat Bheinn
342
Cruach
Rubha na Caillich
Cabrach
Sannaig
Na Cuiltean
Ardfin
Jura Ho.
Am Fraoch Eilean
Rubha na Traille
Brosdale Island
A
R
G
Y
L
L
Cruach Ionnastail
Tarbert Bay
Rubha nam
Ardnackaig
Carsaig Island
Arinafad Beg
Scotnish
Carsaig Bay
Eilean Dubh
Tayvallich
Turbiskill
Kilmory
Eilean Loain
Barrahormid
Taynish
Keillmore
New Ulva
Ulva Islands
Dunrostan
Danna Island
Corr Eilean
Eilean Mor
Kilmory
Kilmory Bay
Point of Knap
Kilberry Head
Kilberry
Rubha Cruitiridh
Loch Stornoway
Ardpatrick Point
Ronachan Point
West Tarbert Bay
Port Mor
East Tarbert Bay
Tarbert
Creag Bhan
100
Ardailly
Druimyeon Bay
Rhunahaorine Point
Gigha Island
Ardminish
Caolas Gigha
Craro Island
Achamore Gardens
Grob Bagh
Cara Island
Mull of Cara
Cnoc Reamhar
265
Bellanoch
Gariob
Knapdale Forest
Seafield
Achnamara
Kilmichael of Inverlussa
Ashfield
Cruach Breacain
360
Cruach Lusach
466
Achaboish
Ellary
Clach-bhreac
Cruach a'Phubeil
477
Stob Odhar
562
Ballyaurgan
Baile Boidheach
Cnoc a Bharaille
Druimdrishaig
Larach na Gaibhre
Dubh Chreag
480
Loch nan Torran
Cretshengan
Meall Reamhar
Dubhchlad
Coulaghailtro
Cruach Airde
Carse
Dunmore
Achadh-chaorrunn
Ardpatrick
Gartnagrenach
Portachoillan
Quinhill
Clachan
Ronachan
Cruach nam Fi
269
Corriechrevie
Ballochroy
Auchinafaud
Cruach Mhic-Gougain
Cnoc-an t-Samhlaidh
Rhunahaorine
Narachan Hill
285
Cnoc Reamhar
Tayinloan
Killean
Sunadale
Grogport
Deucheran Hill
329
Cruach Mhic-an t-Saoir
361
Beacharr
Cruach nam Gabhar
354
Carradale Forest
Achaglass
Muasdale
Diollaid Mhor
426
Rhonadale
Carradale
Glenacardoch Point
Belloch
Arnicle
Beinn Bhreac
Dippen
Barr Water
Glenbarr
Beinn an Tuirc
454
Torrisdale
Bord Mor
408
Whitestone
Bellochantuy Bay
Bellochantuy
Meall Buidhe
374
Saddell
Bunlarie
Saddell Bay
Corrylach
Saddell Forest
Killocraw
Sgreadan Hill
397
Ugadale Point
Tangy Loch
Tangy
Skeroblingarry
Ballochgair
Westport
Low Ballivain
Drumgarve
Glen Lussa
Callyburn
Kilchenzie
Peninver
Machrihanish Bay
Ardnacross Bay
East Darlochan
Kilmichael
Drumore
Campbeltown (Machrihanish)
Campbeltown
Machrihanish
Witchburn
Campbeltown Loch
Davaar Island
Drumlemble
Chiscan
Dalivaddy
Kilkerran
Glenramskill
Davaar
Knocknaha
Beinn Ghuilean
352
Eradale Point
New Orleans
Oatfield
Kilchrist
Chiscan Water
The Slate
385
Killellan
Arinarach Hill
Rubha Duin Bhain
Cnoc Moy
446
Largybaan
Conie Water
Feochaig
Ru Stafnish
Cnoc Reamhar
277
Cnoc Odhar
Glen Kerran
Sheanachie
Breckrie
Brecklate
Glen Breackerie
Kepringan
Kildavie
Strone Glen
Machaarioch
Polliwilline Bay
Beinn na Lice
428
Garveld
Keil
Carrine
Southend
Mull of Kintyre
Feorlan
Carskey Bay
Borgadelmore Point
Sanda Sound
Sheep Island
Sanda Island
Ballycastle (proposed)
A83
B842
B843
B8024
B8025
K
I
N
T
Y
R
E
B
U
T
E
13
15
24
33
52
Sound of Gigha
Kilbrannan Sound

G
H
J
K
L
M
N
63
Lochgilphead
Tighnabruaich
Rothesay
Port Bannatyne
Dunoon
Gourock
GREENOCK
PORT GLASGOW
INVERCLYDE
Helensburgh
Kilcreggan
Cove
WEST DUNBARTONSHIRE
DUMBARTON
CLYDEBANK
Renfrew
RENFREWSHIRE
PAISLEY
Johnstone
Barrhead
EAST RENFREWSHIRE
Largs
Great Cumbrae
Millport
Fairlie
Kilbirnie
Beith
Dalry
Kilwinning
Stewarton
Ardrossan
Saltcoats
Stevenston
Irvine
KILMARNOCK
Troon
Prestwick
AYR
Maybole
Girvan
Dalmellington
ISLE OF ARRAN
Brodick
Lamlash
Lochranza
Holy Island
Pladda
Ailsa
NORTH AYRSHIRE
EAST AYRSHIRE
SOUTH AYRSHIRE
SOUND OF BUTE
FIRTH OF CLYDE
LOCH LOMOND
Irvine Bay
Ayr Bay
Culzean Bay
Heads of Ayr
Turnberry
(summer only)
1
2
3
4
5
6
7
8
9
58
52

63
64
57
52
A
B
C
D
E
F
G
1
2
3
4
5
6
7
8
9
WEST DUNBARTONSHIRE
EAST DUNBARTONSHIRE
INVERCLYDE
RENFREWSHIRE
EAST RENFREWSHIRE
GLASGOW CITY
NORTH AYRSHIRE
EAST AYRSHIRE
SOUTH AYRSHIRE
FIRTH OF CLYDE
LOCH LOMOND
CAMPSIE FELLS
Kilpatrick Hills
Helensburgh
Dumbarton
Greenock
Port Glasgow
Gourock
Dunoon
Rothesay
Largs
Millport
Great Cumbrae
Little Cumbrae
Paisley
Renfrew
Clydebank
Glasgow
Bearsden
Milngavie
Kirkintilloch
Rutherglen
Coatbridge
Hamilton
East Kilbride
Johnstone
Barrhead
Kilmacolm
Kilbirnie
Beith
Dalry
West Kilbride
Ardrossan
Saltcoats
Stevenston
Kilwinning
Irvine
Irvine Bay
Kilmarnock
Stewarton
Kilmaurs
Galston
Newmilns
Darvel
Troon
Prestwick
Ayr
Ayr Bay
Heads of Ayr
Mauchline
Cumnock
New Cumnock
Maybole
Girvan
Dalmellington
Crosshill
Culzean Bay
Holy Island
Lady Isle
Turnberry Bay

KIRKCALDY
DUNFERMLINE
Cowdenbeath
Kinghorn
Burntisland
Inverkeithing
North Queensferry
South Queensferry
CITY OF EDINBURGH
EDINBURGH
Leith
Portobello
Musselburgh
Prestonpans
Cockenzie and Port Seton
Tranent
Dalkeith
Bonnyrigg
Lasswade
Loanhead
Penicuik
MIDLOTHIAN
FIRTH OF FORTH
FALKIRK
Grangemouth
Bo'ness
Linlithgow
Bathgate
Livingston
Armadale
Whitburn
WEST LOTHIAN
PENTLAND HILLS REGIONAL PARK
NORTH LANARKSHIRE
Cumbernauld
AIRDRIE
MOTHERWELL
WISHAW
SOUTH LANARKSHIRE
Lanark
Carluke
Carstairs
Biggar
Abington
Crawford
Leadhills
Wanlockhead
Sanquhar
West Linton
Peebles
Innerleithen
Walkerburn
Traquair
Moffat
Tweedsmuir
Ettrick
Yarrow
Kincardine
Culross
Alloa
Stirling
Denny
Dunipace
Bannockburn
Muirhouses
Kirkliston
Ratho
Broxburn
Uphall
Mid Calder
West Calder
Forth
Douglas
Symington
Skirling
Broughton
Eddleston
Cardrona
Gorebridge
Newtongrange
Rosewell
Carrington
Temple
Howgate
Leadburn
Dolphinton
Carnwath
Newbigging
Elsrickle
Blyth Bridge
Romannobridge
Lyne
Stobo
Drumelzier
Crawfordjohn
Glespin
Roberton
Wiston
Lamington
Coulter
Elvanfoot
Beattock
M8
M9
M74
M90
A74(M)
A702
A701
A72
A7
A68

A
B
C
D
E
F
G
65
54
59
1
2
3
4
5
6
7
8
9
KIRKCALDY
DUNFERMLINE
Cowdenbeath
Kinghorn
Burntisland
Inverkeithing
Rosyth
North Queensferry
South Queensferry
Linlithgow
Bo'ness
Bathgate
Livingston
Uphall
Broxburn
Kirkliston
CITY OF EDINBURGH
EDINBURGH
Leith
Portobello
Musselburgh
Prestonpans
Cockenzie and Port Seton
Tranent
Dalkeith
Bonnyrigg
Lasswade
Loanhead
Penicuik
Balerno
Currie
Juniper Green
MIDLOTHIAN
PENTLAND HILLS REGIONAL PARK
WEST LOTHIAN
EAST LOTHIAN
North Berwick
Gullane
Dirleton
Aberlady
Haddington
East Linton
Gifford
Pencaitland
Ormiston
Gorebridge
Carnwath
Biggar
West Linton
Peebles
Innerleithen
Walkerburn
Galashiels
Melrose
Lauder
Stow
Selkirk
Hawick
Moffat
Broughton
Eddleston
Lamancha
Carlops
Lyne
Kirkton Manor
Clovenfords
Newtown St Boswells
St Boswells
Denholm
Lilliesleaf
Ettrick
Tweedsmuir
Crawford
Abington
FIRTH OF FORTH
Moorfoot Hills
Lammermuir
SCOTTISH BORDERS
TWEEDDALE
ETTRICK FOREST
M8
M9
M90
A1
A7
A68
A70
A71
A72
A701
A702
A703
A708
A74(M)

G
H
J
K
L
M
N
1
2
3
4
5
6
7
8
9
Dunbar
Barns Ness
Skateraw
Skateraw Harbour
Thorntonloch
Innerwick
Cockburnspath
Cove
Reed Point
Siccar Point
Wheat Stack
Telegraph Hill
St Abb's Head
St Abbs
Coldingham
Coldingham Bay
Northfield
Lumsdaine
Eyemouth
Burnmouth
Grantshouse
Houndwood
Reston
Ayton
Cairncross
Abbey St Bathans
Cranshaws
Ellemford
Marygold
Auchencrow
Chirnside
Chirnsidebridge
Preston
Edrom
Duns
Foulden
Mordington
Lamberton
Needles Eye
Sharper's Head
Berwick-upon-Tweed
Tweedmouth
Spittal
Scremerston
Paxton
Hutton
Allanton
Blackadder
Sunwick
Whitelaw
Gavinton
Choicelee
Polwarth
Sinclair's Hill
Whitsome
Fishwick
Horncliffe
Longridge Towers
Ladykirk
Horndean
Norham
Thornton
Shoreswood
Murton
West Allerdean
Ancroft
Grindon
Upsettlington
Swinton
Swintonmill
Simprim
Greenlaw
Fogo
Fogorig
Purves Hall
Leitholm
Eccles
Orange Lane
Coldstream
Cornhill on Tweed
Wark
Lennel
Birgham
Hume
Eastern Howlaws
Humehall
Legars
Sweethope Hill
Stichill
Ednam
Nenthorn
Kelso
Hendersyde Park
Hadden
Carham
East Learmouth
Branxton
Crookham
Pallinsburn House
Etal
Ford
Castle Heaton
Duddo
Felkington
Bowsden
Barmoor Lane End
Lowick
Berrington
Cheswick
Goswick
Cheswick Black Rocks
Beal
West Mains
West Kyloe
Fenwick
Buckton
Kyloe Hills
Emmanuel Head
Holy Island or Lindisfarne
Castle Point
Holy Island Sands
Guile Point
Fenham Flats
Burrows Hole
Ross
Elwick
Budle Point
Budle Bay
Budle
Bamburgh
Inner Sound
Staple Sound
Longstone
Farne Islands
Farne Island
House Rocks
Seahouses
North Sunderland
Beadnell
Beadnell Bay
Benthall
Swinhoe
Tughall
High Newton by-the-Sea
Newton-by-the-Sea
Snook Point
Embleton Bay
Embleton
Dunstan
Craster
Cullernose Point
Howick
Howick Haven
Longhoughton
Boulmer
Boulmer Haven
Lesbury
Alnmouth
Alnmouth Bay
Warkworth
Amble
Coquet
Hauxley
Hauxley Haven
Radcliffe
Togston
North Togston
Hadston Carrs
Chevington Drift
Druridge Bay
West Chevington
Broomhill
Felton
Acklington
Guyzance
Morwick Hall
Shilbottle
High Buston
Alnwick
Denwick
Hawkhill
Rennington
Stamford
Littlehoughton
Rock
Christon Bank
Brunton
Preston
Ellingham
Chathill
North Charlton
South Charlton
Brownieside
Newstead
Newham
Lucker
Adderstone
Warenford
Belford
Middleton
Easington
Waren Mill
Spindlestone
Bradford
Glororum
Burton
Elford
Detchant
Holburn
North Hazelrigg
South Hazelrigg
Warenton
Bellshill
Twizell House
Greendykes
Chatton
Chillingham
Hepburn
Old Bewick
New Bewick
West Ditchburn
Eglingham
Beanley
East Bolton
Shipley
Hulne Park
Bolton
Abberwick
Broome Wood
Edlingham
Whittingham
Thrunton
Callaly
Lorbottle
Lorbottle Hall
Cartington
Snitter
Rothbury
Thropton
Whitton
Newtown
Great Tosson
Hepple
Caistron
Flotterton
Warton
Netherton
Biddlestone
Alwinton
Harbottle
Sharperton
Holystone
Burradon
Linbriggs
Linshiels
Shillmoor
Great Ryle
Little Ryle
Alnham
Scrainwood
Prendwick
Ingram
Reaveley
Brandon
Branton
Powburn
Glanton
Fowberry
Roddam
Wooperton
Ilderton
Roseden
Lilburn Tower
East Lilburn
Newtown
Wooler
Haugh Head
Humbleton
Earle
Middleton Hall
Wandon
Akeld
Coupland
Ewart Newtown
Lanton
Kirknewton
Milfield
Flodden
Kimmerston
Fenton
Nesbit
Doddington
West Horton
East Horton
Howtel
Downham
Pawston
Kilham
Mindrum
Westnewton
Shotton
Kirk Yetholm
Town Yetholm
Hethpool
Langleeford
The Cheviot
Sourhope
Mowhaugh
Hownam
Hownam Mains
Chatto
Swanlaws
Morebattle
Gateshaw
Linton
Frogden
Cessford
Crailing
Crailinghall
Eckford
Nisbet
Heiton
Roxburgh
Maxwellheugh
Lempitlaw
Sprouston
Pressen
Oxnam
Swinside Hall
Mossburnford
Falla
Camptown
Hartrigge
Jedburgh
Blindburn
Makendon
Danger Zone
Catcleugh
Byrness
Redesdale Forest
Kielderhead Moor
Carter Bar
Sills
Rochester
Horsley
North Yardhope
Rushy Knowe
Davyshiel Common
Tosson Hill
Simonside
Forestburn
Longframlington
Pauperhaugh
Swarland
Old Swarland
Newton-on-the-Moor
Thirston
Eshott
NORTHUMBERLAND
CHEVIOT HILLS
55
A1
A1087
A1107
A6105
A6112
A697
A698
A68
A1068
A6089
B6355
B6438
B6437
B6460
B6461
B6470
B6436
B6396
B6397
B6352
B6351
B6350
B6354
B6353
B6525
B6348
B6349
B6346
B6347
B6341
B6342
B6340
B6345
B6344
B6343
B1340
B1339
B6401
B6364

A
B
C
D
E
F
G
1
2
3
4
5
6
7
8
9
67
56
Treshnish Isles
Lunga
Gometra
ULVA
Ulva Ferry
Staffa
Fingal's Cave
Iona
Fionnphort
Bunessan
ROSS OF MULL
Loch Scridain
Loch na Keal
MULL
Ben More
966
Salen
Craignure
Duart Castle
Lochdon
Torosay Castle
Glen More
Loch Buie
Kerrera
FIRTH OF LORN
Garvellachs
Isles of the Sea
Luing
Shuna
Scarba
Torran Rocks
Dubh Artach
COLONSAY
Scalasaig
Kiloran
Oronsay
Oban
Colonsay
Jura
JURA
Sound of Jura
Craighouse
Feolin Ferry
Lagg
Ardlussa
Loch Tarbert
Paps of Jura
ISLAY
Port Askaig
Port Ellen
Bowmore
Port Charlotte
Portnahaven
Bridgend
Ballygrant
Loch Indaal
Laggan Bay
Loch Gruinart
Ardnave Point
Sound of Islay
ARGYLL
KNAPDALE
Knapdale Forest
Loch Sween
Tayvallich
Crinan
Crinan Canal
Lochgilphead
Loch Caolisport
KINTYRE
Tarbert
Gigha Island
Danna Island
Kilberry
A849
A846
A847
A816
A83

G
H
J
K
68
L
M
N
1
2
3
4
5
6
7
8
9
64
57
ARGYLL AND BUTE
LOCH LOMOND
REGIONAL PARK
QUEEN ELIZABETH FOREST PARK
ARGYLL FOREST PARK
WEST DUNBARTONSHIRE
RENFREWSHIRE
INVERCLYDE
EAST RENFREWS
FIRTH OF CLYDE
SOUND OF BUTE
Inveraray
Lochgilphead
Dunoon
Rothesay
GREENOCK
PORT GLASGOW
Gourock
Helensburgh
DUMBARTON
Largs
Millport
Kilcreggan
Arrochar
Aberfoyle
Tyndrum
Dalmally
Taynuilt
Lochgoilhead
Strachur
Tighnabruaich
Balloch
Alexandria
Drymen
CLYDEBANK
PAISLEY
Johnstone
Bearsden
Milngavie
Barrhead
Renfrew
Callander
Crianlarich
Killin
Loch Fyne
Loch Long
Loch Katrine
Loch Awe
Loch Striven
Skelmorlie
Wemyss Bay
West Kilbride
Kilbirnie
Lochwinnoch
Cove
Crosbie
Dalry
Beith
Kilmacolm
Bridge of Weir
Erskine
Ardlui
Tarbet
Luss
Garelochhead
Tarbert
Clachan of Glendaruel
Glendaruel
Otter Ferry
Colintraive
Kames
Portavadie
Ardentinny
Cairndow
Ardrishaig
Crinan
Kilmartin
Ford
Lochgoilhead
Innellan
Toward
Ardgartan
Rest and be thankful
Beinn Ime
Ben Lui
Ben Lomond
Ben Vorlich
Ben More
Ben Cruachan
Lochawe
Kilchurn Castle
Inverarnan
Rowardennan
Dalavich
Kilmelford
Furnace
Minard
Strone Point
Rosneath
Shandon
Rhu
Cardross
Kippen
Gartmore
Stronachlachar
Inversnaid
Bowling
Old Kilpatrick
Houston
Linwood
Elderslie
Neilston
Uplawmoor
Howwood
Kilbarchan
Cumbrae
Great Cumbrae
Little Cumbrae
Fairlie
Hunterston
Kilchattan Bay
Port Bannatyne
Ascog
Ettrick Bay
Inchmarnock
Lochranza

A
B
C
D
E
F
G
1
2
3
4
5
6
7
8
9
69
63
58
59
PERTH AND KINROSS
STIRLING
THE CLACKMANNANSHIRE
FALKIRK
WEST DUNBARTONSHIRE
EAST DUNBARTONSHIRE
NORTH LANARKSHIRE
RENFREWSHIRE
GLASGOW CITY
EAST RENFREWSHIRE
QUEEN ELIZABETH FOREST PARK
LOCH LOMOND
Loch Tay
Loch Earn
Loch Katrine
Killin
Crieff
Callander
Aberfoyle
Doune
Dunblane
Bridge of Allan
STIRLING
Alloa
Tillicoultry
Dollar
Auchterarder
Comrie
Lochearnhead
Balquhidder
Kenmore
Drymen
Balloch
DUMBARTON
Milngavie
Bearsden
CLYDEBANK
Kirkintilloch
CUMBERNAULD
Kilsyth
Denny
Grangemouth
Bo'ness
Linlithgow
Bathgate
Armadale
Whitburn
AIRDRIE
COATBRIDGE
GLASGOW
Renfrew
PAISLEY
Johnstone
Barrhead
RUTHERGLEN
EAST KILBRIDE
HAMILTON
MOTHERWELL
WISHAW
Kincardine
Culross
Gleneagles
Blackford
Kippen
Fintry
Campsie Fells
Kilpatrick Hills
Ochil Hills

G
H
J
K
L
M
N
70
71
60
61
1
2
3
4
5
6
7
8
9
ANGUS
DUNDEE CITY
DUNDEE
Arbroath
Carnoustie
Monifieth
Broughty Ferry
Tayport
Newport-on-Tay
FIRTH OF TAY
Tentsmuir Forest
PERTH
Bridgend
Scone
Newburgh
St Andrews
Cupar
Auchtermuchty
Ladybank
Falkland
FIFE
Kinross
Loch Leven
GLENROTHES
Markinch
Leslie
Leven
Methil
Buckhaven
Crail
Kingsbarns
Anstruther
Pittenweem
St Monans
Elie
Earlsferry
KIRKCALDY
Dysart
Burntisland
Kinghorn
Cowdenbeath
Lochgelly
Inverkeithing
North Queensferry
South Queensferry
FIRTH OF FORTH
North Berwick
EAST LOTHIAN
Dunbar
Haddington
Tranent
Prestonpans
Cockenzie and Port Seton
Musselburgh
CITY OF EDINBURGH
EDINBURGH
Leith
Portobello
Dalkeith
Bonnyrigg
Lasswade
MIDLOTHIAN
Penicuik
PENTLAND HILLS REGIONAL PARK
LAMMERMUIR HILLS
Gifford
East Linton
Aberlady
Gullane
Lauder
M90
M9
M8
A1
A92
A91
A90

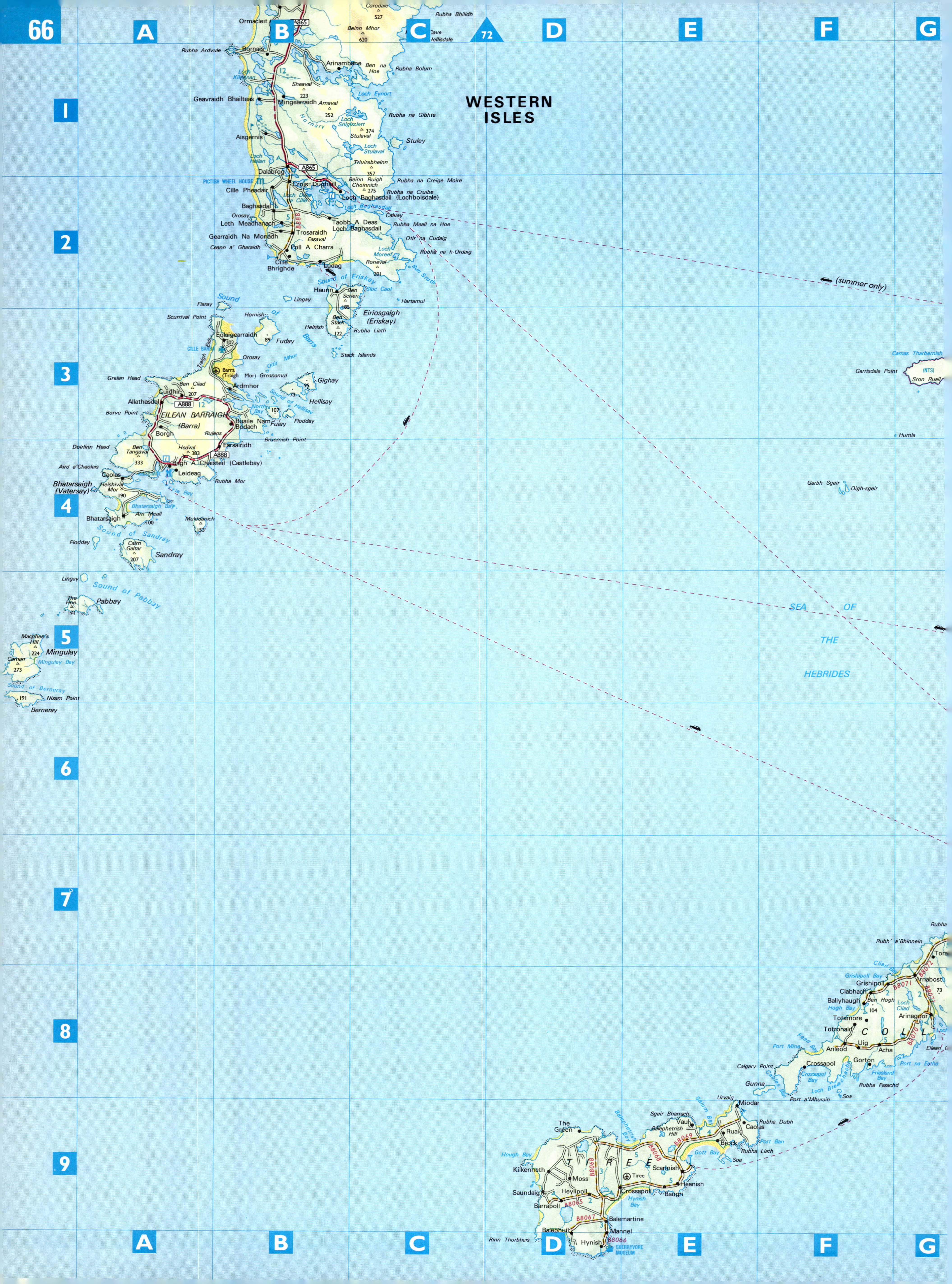
WESTERN ISLES
SEA OF THE HEBRIDES
Ormacleit
Bornais
Arinambane
Rubha Ardvule
Loch Kildonan
Geavraidh Bhailteas
Mingearraidh
Aisgernis
Dalabrog
Cros Dughaill
Cille Pheadair
Loch Baghasdail (Lochboisdale)
Baghasdal
Orosay
Leth Meadhanach
Taobh A Deas Loch Baghasdail
Gearraidh Na Monadh
Trosaraidh
Eaasval
Ceann a' Gharaidh
Poll A Charra
Cille Bhrighde
Ludag
Calvay
Rubha Meall na Hoe
Otir na Cudaig
Rubha na h-Ordaig
Rubha na Creige Moire
Rubha na Cruibe
Rubha Bolum
Rubha na Gibhte
Stuley
Loch Eynort
Sheaval
Arnaval
Stulaval
Loch Stulaval
Triuirebheinn
Beinn Ruigh Choinnich
Beinn Mhor
Corodale
Rubha Bhilidh
Cave
Hellisdale
Ben na Hoe
Roneval
Loch Moreef
Ban Sruth
PICTISH WHEEL HOUSE
Sound of Eriskay
Haunn
Ben Scrien
Sloc Caol
Hartamul
Eiriosgaigh (Eriskay)
Ben Stack
Rubha Liath
Heinish
Lingay
Stack Islands
Sound of Barra
Fiaray
Scurrival Point
Hornish
Eolaigearraidh
Fuday
CILLE BARRA
Orosay
Oitir Mhor
Barra (Traigh Mor)
Greanamul
Gighay
Hellisay
Grean Head
Ben Cliad
Cuidhir
Ardmhor
Allathasdal
Borve Point
EILEAN BARRAIGH (Barra)
Borgh
Buaile Nam Bodach
Fuiay
Flodday
Northbay
Sound of Hellisay
Bruernish Point
Doirlinn Head
Ben Tangaval
Heaval
Earsairidh
Rueos
Bagh A Chaisteil (Castlebay)
Leideag
Aird a'Chaolais
Caolas
Rubha Mor
Bhatarsaigh (Vatersay)
Heishival Mor
Vatersay Bay
Bhatarsaigh
Am Meall
Muldoanich
Sound of Sandray
Flodday
Cairn Galtar
Sandray
Lingay
Sound of Pabbay
The Hoe
Pabbay
Macphee's Hill
Mingulay
Carnan
Mingulay Bay
Sound of Berneray
Nisam Point
Berneray
(summer only)
Camas Tharbernish
Garrisdale Point
Sron Ruail
Humla
Garbh Sgeir
Oigh-sgeir
Rubha
Rubh' a'Bhinnein
Cliad Bay
Grishipoll Bay
Grishipoll
Arinabost
Clabhach
Hogh Bay
Ballyhaugh
Ben Hogh
Loch Cliad
Totamore
Arinagour
Totronald
COLL
Uig
Feall Bay
Port Mine
Arileod
Acha
Eilean
Crossapol
Gorton
Port na Eatha
Calgary Point
Crossapol Bay
Friesland Bay
Gunna
Loch Breachacha
Rubha Fasachd
Port a'Mhurain
Soa
Urvaig
Miodar
Salum Bay
Sgeir Bharrach
Vaul
Rubha Dubh
The Green
Balephetrish Hill
Caolas
Ruaig
Port Ban
Brock
Rubha Liath
Gott Bay
Soa
Hough Bay
Kilkenneth
TIREE
Moss
Tiree
Scarinish
Heanish
Saundaig
Heylipoll
Crossapol
Hynish Bay
Baugh
Barrapol
Balemartine
Balephuil
Mannel
Rinn Thorbhais
Hynish
SKERRYVORE MUSEUM
Balephetrish Bay
A865
A888
B888
B8065
B8066
B8067
B8068
B8069
B8070
B8071
B8072
72
A B C D E F G
1 2 3 4 5 6 7 8 9

G
H
J
K
L
M
N
73
68
62
1
2
3
4
5
6
7
8
9
Talisker
Carbost
Drynoch
Sligachan
Sconser
Luib
Dunan
Broadford
Breakish
Kyle of Lochalsh
Kyleakin
Balmacara
Dornie
Ardelve
Glenelg
Shiel Bridge
Kylerhea
Bernera
Eilanreach
Sandaig
Camasunary
Kilmarie
Elgol
Soay
Drinan
Kirkibost
Torrin
Heast
Drumfearn
Duisdealmor
Isle Ornsay
Ord
Tokavaig
Tarskavaig
Achnacloich
Teangue
Kilmore
Kilbeg
Armadale
Ardvasar
Calligarry
Aird of Sleat
Ard Thurinish
Point of Sleat
CUILLIN SOUND
SOUND OF SLEAT
LOCH HOURN
Arnisdale
Corran
Kinloch Hourn
Barrisdale
Inverguseran
Airor
KNOYDART
Inverie
Aultvoulin
Mallaigvaig
Mallaig
Glasnacardoch
Morar
Bracora
Bracorina
Stoul
Kylesknoydart
Kylesmorar
Tarbet
Swordland
NORTH MORAR
LOCH MORAR
Kinlochmorar
Portnaluchaig
Back of Keppoch
Arisaig
Rhumach
Druimindarroch
SOUTH MORAR
Meoble
Kinlochbeoraid
ARISAIG
Arienskill
Lochailort
Inverailort
Glenfinnan
Ardnish
Sanday
Canna Harbour
Kilmory
Kinloch
RUM (RHUM)
Harris
Sound of Canna
SOUND OF RUM
Cleadale
EIGG
Kildonnan
Galmisdale
Sound of Eigg
Port Mor
Muck
Sound of Arisaig
Roshven
Smirisary
MOIDART
Kinlochmoidart
Eilean Shona
Dorlin
Kylesbeg
Glenuig
Ardtoe
Newton of Ardtoe
Shielfoot
Kentra
Acharacle
Ardshealach
Arivegaig
Salen
Resipole
Kilchoan
Ormsaigmore
Sanna
Achosnich
Portuairk
Grigadale
Fascadale
Achateny
Kilmory
Ockle
Swordle
Branault
Point of Ardnamurchan
ARDNAMURCHAN
Glenborrodale
Glenbeg
Laga
Ardslignish
Camphouse
Tarbert
Ardery
Woodend
Ranachan
Strontian
Anaheilt
Scotstown
Polloch
SUNART
Liddesdale
Achleek
Glencripesdale
HIGHLAND
MORVERN
Achagavel
Lochuisge
Achranich
Beach
Kinloch
Rahoy
Barr
Achleanan
Drimnin
Durinemast
Rhemore
Killundine
Claggan
Larachbeg
Ardtornish
Lochaline
Inninbeg
Fiunary
Fiunary Forest
Achnaha
Tobermory
Mishnish
Dervaig
Calgary
Langamull
Croig
Achnadrish
Aros
Lettermore
Ardnacross
Ensay
Treshnish
Tostarie
Kilninian
Ballygown
Kilbrennan
Fanmore
Lagganulva
Achronich
Killiechronan
Salen
Pennygown
Killbeg
Gruline
Killiemor
ULVA
Gometra
Fishnish
Garmony
Scallastle
SOUND OF MULL
LOCH LINNHE
Lismore
Achnacroish
Port Ramsay
Kilcheran
Balure
Benderloch
Port Appin
Appin
Glensanda
Kingairloch
Camasnacroise
Glengalmadale
Drumfern
Conchra
Camus-luinie
Bundalloch
Nostie
Ardintoul
Letterfearn
Totaig
Achnaha
Achnacraig
Ardnastang

A
B
C
D
E
F
G
74
67
63
1
2
3
4
5
6
7
8
9
Kyle of Lochalsh
Kyleakin
Broadford
Breakish
Balmacara
Dornie
Ardelve
Kirkton
Carnach
Loch Duich
Glenelg
Bernera
Kylerhea
Shiel Bridge
Kintail Forest
Five Sisters
Glen Shiel
Cluanie Forest
Loch Cluanie
Glen Affric
Tomich
Fasnakyle Forest
Glen Moriston
Torgyle
Dalchreichart
Dundreggan
Tomchrasky
Bun Loyne
Glen Loyne
Invergarry
Glen Garry
Loch Garry
Tomdoun
Inchlaggan
Greenfield
Loch Quoich
Kinloch Hourn
Loch Hourn
Arnisdale
Corran
Sandaig
Knoydart
Inverie
Airor
Loch Nevis
Mallaig
Morar
North Morar
Loch Morar
Tarbet
Glendessary
Strathan
Loch Arkaig
Achnasaul
Clunes
Loch Lochy
Laggan
Glen Loy
Gairlochy
Spean Bridge
Roybridge
Tirindrish
Glenfinnan
Kinlocheil
Fassfern
Loch Eil
Corpach
Banavie
Caol
Fort William
Ben Nevis
Claggan
Lochaber
Loch Linnhe
Onich
North Ballachulish
Kinlochleven
Glencoe
Ballachulish
Rannoch Moor
Kingshouse Hotel
Buachaille Etive Mor
Loch Etive
Glen Etive
Dalness
Duror
Kentallen
Appin
Port Appin
Portnacroish
Kinlochlaich
Barcaldine
Benderloch
Ledaig
Lismore
Loch Creran
Kilmalieu
Glengalmadale
Inversanda
Ardgour
Corran
Clovullin
Strontian
Loch Sunart
Salen
Acharacle
Moidart
Kinlochmoidart
Glenuig
Lochailort
Arisaig
Loch Ailort
Sunart
Morvern
Lochaline
Ardtornish
Drimnin
Kilchoan
Ardnamurchan
Sound of Sleat
Sleat
Loch Aline
Lynn of Lorn
Sound of Mull
A87
A830
A82
A861
A884
A828
A86
A851
A890
A887

G
H
J
K
L
M
N
75
64
70
2
3
4
5
6
7
8
9
HIGHLAND
MOUNTAINS
MONADHLIATH
GRAMPIAN
MOUNTAINS
BADENOCH
PERTH AND KINROSS
GLENMORE FOREST PARK
CAIRNGORM MOUNTAINS
TAY FOREST PARK
ATHOLL
Loch Ness
Loch Rannoch
Loch Tummel
Loch Tay
Loch Ericht
Loch Laggan
Fort Augustus
Invermoriston
Drumnadrochit
Foyers
Whitefield
Tomatin
Carrbridge
Boat of Garten
Nethy Bridge
Grantown-on-Spey
Aviemore
Coylumbridge
Kincraig
Kingussie
Newtonmore
Laggan
Dalwhinnie
Blair Atholl
Killiecrankie
Pitlochry
Moulin
Aberfeldy
Kenmore
Struan
Calvine
Kinloch Rannoch
Trinafour
Tummel Bridge
Bridge of Gaur
Bridge of Ericht
Dunkeld
Ballinluig
Grandtully
Glen Garry
Glen Lyon
Strathspey
Ben Alder
Ben Macdui
Cairn Gorm
A9
A86
A82
A889
A95
A938
A939
A827
A826
A822
A923
B8019
B846
B847
B970
B851
B862

A
B
C
D
E
F
G
1
2
3
4
5
6
7
8
9
76
69
64
65
MORAY
ABER
Grantown-on-Spey
Carrbridge
Boat of Garten
Aviemore
Kingussie
Newtonmore
Kincraig
Nethy Bridge
Tomintoul
Tomnavoulin
Glenlivet
Cromdale
Dulnain Bridge
Coylumbridge
Inverdruie
GLENMORE FOREST PARK
CAIRNGORM MOUNTAINS
Cairn Gorm
Ben Macdui
Braeriach
Cairngorms
Loch Morlich
Braemar
Crathie
Balmoral
Inverey
Lochnagar
Glenshee
Spittal of Glenshee
Blair Atholl
Killiecrankie
Pitlochry
Aberfeldy
Kenmore
Dunkeld
Blairgowrie
Rattray
Alyth
Coupar Angus
Kirkmichael
Bridge of Cally
Ballinluig
Strathtay
Grandtully
Weem
Tummel Bridge
Trinafour
Dalwhinnie
Struan
Calvine
TAY FOREST PARK
Loch Tummel
Loch Rannoch
Kinloch Rannoch
Forest of Atholl
ATHOLL
Gaick Lodge
Bridge of Dee
Glenfeshie Forest
Feshiebridge
Insh
Ruthven
Kincraig
Laggan

ABERDEEN
CITY
ABERDEEN
Stonehaven
Inverbervie
Laurencekirk
Montrose
Brechin
Forfar
Arbroath
Banchory
Peterculter
Inverurie
Oldmeldrum
Kintore
Ellon
Alford
Aboyne
Ballater
Torphins
Dyce
Westhill
Edzell
Johnshaven
Gourdon
Portlethen
Newtonhill
Kemnay
Insch
Rhynie
Strachan
Fettercairn
Marykirk
Letham
Carnoustie
HOWE O' THE MEARNS
Stromness, Lerwick, & Torshavn
Bergen (summer only)
G
H
J
K
L
M
N
1
2
3
4
5
6
7
8
9
77
65

WESTERN ISLES
UIBHIST A TUATH
(NORTH UIST)
BEINN NA FAOGHLA
(BENBECULA)
UIBHIST A DEAS
(South Uist)
SOUTH HARRIS
LITTLE MINCH
SOUND OF HARRIS
Sound of Pabbay
Sound of Shillay
Sound of Monach
Sound of Eriskay
Sound of Barra
Sound of Taransay
TARBERT
Tairbeart (Tarbert)
Aird Asaig
Urgha
Carragrich
Sgeotasaigh
Caolas Scalpaigh
East Loch Tarbert
Meaghag
Greosabhagh
Scadabhagh
Rubha Bocaig
Cluer
Rubha Cluer
Leac a' Li
Liceasto
Aird Mhige
Manais
Ard Manish
Fleoideabhagh
Cuidhtinis
Rubha Quidnish
Aird Mhighe
Boirseam
Ceann A Bhaigh
Lingarabay Island
Roghadal
ST CLEMENT'S CHURCH
Rubha Vallarip
Renish Point
Strannda
Cairminis
An t-Ob
Taobh Tuath
Traigh na Cleavag
Sgarasta Mhor
Maodal
Chaipaval
Bleaval
Heileasbhal Mor
An Coileach
Roneval
Stronceval
Seilebost
Losgaintir
Beinn Dhubh
Beesdale
Ceann Reamhar
South Harris Forest
Corran Seilebost
Clett Nisabost
Buirgh
Bulabhall
Paibie
Aird Vanish
Rubha Sgeirigin
Rubha Romagi
Ben Raah
Toe Head
Rubha Mas a'Chnuic
Ensay
Killegray
Shillay
Pabbay
Beinn a' Charnain
Baile na Cille
Quinish
Eilean Bhearnaraigh (Berneray)
Boreray
Borgh
Ruisigearraidh
Massacamber
Borve Hill
Groay
Gilsay
Lingay
Scaravay
Port Nan Long
Newton
Aird Thormaid
Beinn Mhor
Stromay
Hermetray
Leac na Hoe
Scarts Rock
Lochportan
Loch Na Madadh (Lochmaddy)
Blathaisbhal
Trumaisge Arraidh
Greinetobht
Oronsay
Huilish Point
Veilish Point
Vallay
Griminis Point
Scolpaig
Balelone
Baile Mhartainn
Hosta
Tigh A Ghearraidh
Hogha Gearraidh
Manish Point
Causamul
Baile Raghaill
Rubha Port Scolpaig
Paibeil
Baile Mor
Ceann A Bhaigh
Cladach A Chaolais
Cladach Chircebost
Oitir Mhor
Kirkibost Island
Rubha Raouill
Deasker
Heisker or Monach Islands
Shillay
Ceann Iar
Ceann Ear
Stockay
Scrot Mor
Haskeir Island
Haskeir Eagach
Solas
Malacleit
Botarua
Marrival
Maari
Crogary Mor
Langais
Saighdinis
Sàmhla
Teanamachar
Baleshare
Corunna
Cairinis
Eaval
North Lee
South Lee
Rubha Mhic Gille-mhicheil
Eigneig Mhor
Eigneig Bheag
Floddaybeg
Floddaymore
Ronaigh (Ronay)
Rubha na Rodagrich
Baile Glas
Griomasaigh (Grimsay)
Ceallan
Uachdar
Benbecula (Baile A Mhanaich)
Baile A Mhanaich (Balivanich)
Aird
Gramsdal
Baile nan Cailleach
Garry-a-siar
Rueval
Griminis
Torlum
Lionacleit
Uisgebhagh
Rubha Cam nan Gall
Creag Ghoraidh
Hornish Point
Ardivachar Point
Aird A Mhachair
Clachan
Iochdar
Wiay
Geirninis
Drimore
Groigearraidh
Stadhlaigearraidh
Ben Tarbert
Loch Sgioport
Ormish Island
Tobha Mor
Snishival
Peighinn nan Aoireann
Staoinebrig
Rubha Aird-mhicheil
Ormacleit
Hecla
Ben Corodale
Beinn Mhor
Rubha Rossel
Rubha Bhilidh
Prince's Cave
Rubha Hellisdale
Rubha Ardvule
Bornais
Arinambane
Ben na Hoe
Rubha Bolum
Sheaval
Geavraidh Bhailteas
Mingearraidh
Arnaval
Rubha na Gibhte
Stulaval
Stuley
Aisgernis
Triuirebheinn
Dalabrog
PICTISH WHEEL HOUSE
Cille Pheadair
Beinn Ruigh Choinnich
Rubha na Creige Moire
Rubha na Cruibe
Loch Baghasdail (Lochboisdale)
Baghasdail
Orosay
Leth Meadhanach
Taobh A Deas Loch Baghasdail
Calvay
Rubha Meall na Hoe
Gearraidh Na Monadh
Trosaraidh
Easaval
Ceann a' Gharaidh
Poll A Charra
Cille Bhrighde
Ludag
Rubha na h-Ordaig
Roneval
Haunn
Ben Scrien
Eiriosgaigh (Eriskay)
Sloc Caol
Hartamul
Ben Stack
Heinish
Rubha Liath
Lingay
Fiaray
Scurrival Point
Hornish
Eolaigearraidh
Fuday
CILLE BARRA
(summer only)
Vaternish
Trumpan
Ardmore Point
Isay Island
Dunvegan Head
Lampay Islands
Galtrigill
Borreraig
Husabost
Feriniquarrie
Totaig
Loch Dunvegan
Milovaig
Oisgill Bay
Waterstein Head
Neist Point
Moonen Bay
COLBOST FOLK MUSEUM
Colbost
Skinidin
Beinn na Creiche
Ben Corkeval
Healabhal Mhor (Macleod's Table North)
Healabhal Bheag (Macleod's Table South)
Ramasaig
Ramasaig Bay
Hoe Rape
The Hoe
Lorgill
Ben Connan
An Dubh Sgeir
MacLeod's Maidens
A865
A867
A859
B893
B894
B892
B891
B890
B888
78
66
A B C D E F G
1 2 3 4 5 6 7 8 9

G
H
J
K
79
L
M
N
Shiant Islands
Eilean Mhuire
Eilean an Tighe
Greenstone Point
Opinan
Mellon Udrigle
Gruinard Bay
Gruinard Island
Achgarve
Laide
First Coast
Second Coast
Little Gruinard
Mellon Charles
Ormiscaig
Aultbea
Isle of Ewe
Drumchork
Rubha Reidh
Cove
Loch Ewe
Melvaig
Aultgrishan
Inverasdale
Midtown
Tournaig
Peterburn
Naast
Boor
Poolewe
Inverewe
North Erradale
Big Sand
Mial
Longa Island
Carn Dearg
Gairloch
Auchtercairn
Gair Loch
Charlestown
Kerrysdale
Port Henderson
Opinan
Badachro
Shieldaig
South Erradale
Redpoint
Talladale
Slattadale
Red Point
Loch Torridon
Fearnmore
Craig
Lower Diabaig
Upper Diabaig
Alligin Shuas
Inveralligin
Beinn Alligin
Torridon
Fasag
Upper Loch Torridon
Fearnbeg
Arinacrinachd
Cuaig
Kenmore
Kalnakill
Lonbain
Inverbain
Ardheslaig
Shieldaig
Balgy
Ben-damph Forest
Glensheildaig Forest
Applecross Forest
Hartfield
Applecross
Milton
Camusteel
Camusterrach
Culduie
Toscaig
Uags
Russel
Ardarroch
Lochcarron
Achintraid
Stromemore
Ardaneaskan
Plockton
Achmore
Stromeferry
Drumbuie
Duirinish
Erbusaig
Badicaul
Kyle of Lochalsh
Kyleakin
Balmacara
Kirkton
Nostie
Ardelve
Dornie
Conchra
Bundalloch
Loch Duich
Inverinate
Letterfearn
Ardintoul
Kylerhea
Bernera
Glenelg
Eilanreach
Balvraid
Sandaig
Sandaig Islands
Arnisdale
Loch Hourn
Shiel Bridge
Glen More
Rona
Dry Harbour
Eilean Tigh
Eilean Fladday
Torran
Arnish
Brochel
Manish Point
Raasay
Inner Sound
Sound of Raasay
Glame
Balachuirn
Oskaig
Clachan
Inverarish
East Suisnish
Suisnish Point
Holoman Bay
Crowlin Islands
Longay
Scalpay
Pabay
Broadford
Broadford Bay
Harrapool
Skulamus
Breakish
Lower Breakish
Upper Breakish
Sconser
Luib
Dunan
Torrin
Kilbride
Strathaird
Camasunary
Kirkibost
Kilmarie
Elgol
Drinan
Glasnakille
Soay
Soay Sound
Loch Scavaig
Cuillin
Cuillin Hills
Loch Eishort
Ord
Tokavaig
Tarskavaig
Achnacloich
Isleornsay
Eilean Iarmain
Duisdealmor
Camus Croise
Kilmore
Sleat
Inverguseran
Heast
Drumfearn
Kyle Rhea
Trotternish
Rubha Hunish
Duntulm
Kilmaluag
Duntulm Bay
Tulm Island
Flodigarry
Hunglader
Kilmuir
Kilvaxter
Balgown
Monkstadt
Digg
Staffin
Staffin Bay
Staffin Island
Stenscholl
Maligar
Marishader
Elishader
Garros
Culnaknock
Lealt
Rigg
Idrigil
Uig
Uig Bay
Earlish
Balnaknock
Cuidrach
Peinlich
Glenuachdarach
Kingsburgh
Eyre
Kensaleyre
Snizort
Loch Snizort
Lyndale Point
Lynedale
Treaslane
Flashader
Greshornish
Edinbain
Bernisdale
Tote
Skeabost
Carbost
Borve
Drumuie
Uigshader
Glengrasco
Portree
Torvaig
Penifiler
Camastianavaig
Glenmore
Mugeary
Lower Ollach
Upper Ollach
Peinchorran
Sligachan
Glen Sligachan
Drynoch
Glen Drynoch
Carbost
Talisker
Talisker Bay
Eynort
Minginish
Glenbrittle
Cuilinmean
Loch Brittle
Skye
Bracadale
Struan
Coillore
Ullinish
Balmore
Ose
Harlosh
Vatten
Dunvegan
Roag
Lusta
Colbost
Fernilea
Portnalong
Oronsay
Wiay
Loch Harport
Loch Bracadale
Ascrib Islands
Fladda-chuain
Gaeilavore Island
Gearran Island
Eilean Trodday
Eilean Flodigarry
Rubha Bhrollum
Scalpaigh
A87
A850
A855
A863
A832
A896
A890
A851
A87
B8009
B8083
B8021
B8056
Pabay
Sound of Shiant
Compass
67

A
B
C
79
D
E
F
G
1
2
3
4
5
6
7
8
9
73
68
Ullapool
Loch Broom
Gruinard Bay
Greenstone Point
Rubha Reidh
Loch Ewe
Poolewe
Gairloch
Gair Loch
Loch Maree
Kinlochewe
Beinn Eighe
Liathach
Beinn Alligin
Upper Loch Torridon
Loch Torridon
Torridon
Shieldaig
Applecross Forest
Applecross
Lochcarron
Loch Carron
Plockton
Kyle of Lochalsh
Kyleakin
Broadford Bay
Balmacara
Dornie
Loch Duich
Shiel Bridge
Five Sisters
Kintail Forest
Glen Shiel
Loch Alsh
Glenelg
Loch Hourn
Sound of Sleat
Inner Sound
Achnasheen
Strath Bran
Ledgowan Forest
Achnashellach Forest
Strathconon
Glen Affric
Cannich
Glen Cannich
Loch Mullardoch
Monar Forest
East Monar Forest
Fannich Forest
Loch Fannich
Braemore
Strathvaich Forest
Inverlael Forest
Rhidorroch Forest
Dundonnell
Gruinard Forest
Letterewe
Fisherfield Forest
Flowerdale Forest
Shieldaig Forest
Coulin Forest
Attadale Forest
West Monar Forest
Killilan Forest
Cluanie Forest
Glen Cluanie
Lundie
Dalchreichart
Torgyle
Glen Moriston
W E S T E R   R O S S
H I G H L A N D
A832
A835
A890
A896
A87
A887
A851
B8021
B8056

G
H
J
K
L
M
N
80
76
69
1
2
3
4
5
6
7
8
9
Invercassley
Oykel Bridge
Langwell
Strath Oykel
Rosehall
Auchinduich
Altass
Linsidemore
Invershin
Achinduich
Lairg
Pittentrail
Rogart
Dalnamain
Little Torboll
Dornoch
Embo
Golspie
Skelbo
Littleferry
Dornoch Firth
Bonar Bridge
Ardgay
Spinningdale
Clashmore
Edderton
Tain
Portmahomack
Tarbat Ness
Wilkhaven
Inver
Balintore
Shandwick
Nigg
Invergordon
Alness
Cromarty
Cromarty Firth
Dingwall
Strathpeffer
Conon Bridge
Muir of Ord
Beauly
Beauly Firth
Black Isle
Fortrose
Rosemarkie
Avoch
Nairn
Forres
Ardersier
Inverness
Moray Firth
Culloden
Cawdor
Croy
Drumnadrochit
Loch Ness
Invermoriston
Fort Augustus
Glendoebeg
Dores
Inverfarigaig
Foyers
Whitebridge
Carrbridge
Aviemore
Grantown-on-Spey
Glenmore Forest Park
Tomatin
Moy
Daviot
Highland
Strathdearn
Strathglass
Strathconon
Strathcarron
Easter Ross
Monadhliath Mountains
Cairngorm Mountains
Glenmore Lodge
Kingussie
Dulnain Bridge
Nethy Bridge
Boat of Garten
Coylumbridge
Rothiemurchus
A9
A96
A82
A835
A862
A832
A836
A949
A939
A940
A938
A95
A887
A833
A831
B9176
B9175
B9163
B9006
B9091
B852
B862
B861
B851
Danger Zone

A
B
C
D
E
F
G
81
70
75
1
2
3
4
5
6
7
8
9
MORAY
FIRTH
MORAY
GLENMORE FOREST PARK
CAIRNGORM MOUNTAINS
Tarbat Ness
Portmahomack
Wilkhaven
Hilton
Bindal
Rockfield
Inver
Tarrel
Balintore
Shandwick
Hilton of Cadboll
Cadboll
Geanies Ho.
Kirkwall
Halliman Skerries
Covesea Skerries
Clashach Point
Burghead
Burghead Bay
Stotfield
Branderburgh
Lossiemouth
LOSSIEMOUTH FISHERIES & COMMUNITIES MUS
Hopeman
Gordonstoun
Cummingston
Roseisle
Duffus
Salterhill
Spynie Canal
Findrassie
Bishopmill
Elgin
Findhorn
Kinloss
Hempriggs
Coltfield
Muirhead
Alves
Miltonhill
Forres
Nairn
Culbin Forest
Welhill
Kintessack
Moy House
Dyke
Kingsteps
Auldearn
Newton of Dalvey
Rafford
Califer
Tulloch
Pittendreich
Miltonduff
Longmorn
Thornhill
Dallas
Rothes
Craigellachie
Charlestown of Aberlour
Dufftown
Keith
Buckie
Portgordon
Findochty
Portknockie
Cullen
Spey Bay
Kingston
Garmouth
Fochabers
Mosstodloch
Urquhart
Lhanbryde
Boat o' Brig
Mulben
Newmill
Grange Crossroads
Drybridge
Rathven
Portessie
Ianstown
Seatown
Clochan
Drummuir
Botriphnie
Mulben
Auchindoun
Glenlivet
Tomintoul
Tomnavoulin
Bridge of Avon
Dalchirach
Ballindalloch
Advie
Cromdale
Grantown-on-Spey
Speybridge
Carrbridge
Boat of Garten
Nethy Bridge
Aviemore
Coylumbridge
Kincraig
Dulnain Bridge
Skye of Curr
Duthil
Dava
Ferness
Cawdor
Lochindorb
Glenmore Lodge
Rhynie
Lumsden
Kildrummy
Strathdon
Cock Bridge
Corgarff
Tornahaish
Huntly
A96
A95
A939
A941
A940
A920
A97
A98
A938
A942
A944
A990
B9010
B9012
B9013
B9015
B9016
B9018
B9102
B9103
B9136
B9153
B9007
B9008
B9009
B9014
B9115
B9002
B9089
B9101
B9090
B9176
Ben Rinnes
Ben Aigan
Carn Kitty
Hill of Stob
Cairn Cattoch
Blackwater Forest
Glen Fiddich Forest
Glen Livet
Hills of Cromdale
Ladder Hills
Speymouth Forest
Darnaway Forest
Lossie Forest
Innes Canal
Danger Zone
Spey Mouth

G
H
J
K
L
M
N
1
2
3
4
5
6
7
8
9
Portsoy
Whitehills
Banff
Macduff
Gardenstown
Crovie
Troup Head
Rosehearty
Sandhaven
Fraserburgh
Kinnairds Head
Inverallochy
St Combs
Strathbeg Bay
Rattray Head
Rattray Bay
Aberchirder
Turriff
New Pitsligo
Strichen
New Deer
Maud
Mintlaw
Longside
Peterhead
Boddam
Cruden Bay
Bay of Cruden
Port Erroll
Whinnyfold
Ellon
Newburgh
Oldmeldrum
Inverurie
Kintore
Dyce
Fyvie
Cuminestown
Huntly
Insch
Kemnay
Alford
Balmedie
Potterton
Udny Green
Pitmedden
Tarves
Methlick
Auchnagatt
Hatton
Stuartfield
Old Deer
Fetterangus
Mormond Hill
Danger Zone
Scotstown Head
Kirkton Head
Buchan Ness
Murdoch Head
Newburgh Bar
Blackdog Rock
North Tarbothill
Bridge of Don
ABERDEEN CITY
ABERDEEN
Stromness, Lerwick & Torshavn
Bergen (summer only)
A90
A98
A947
A948
A950
A952
A96
A920
A975
A981
A982
71

A
B
C
D
E
F
G
1
2
3
4
5
6
7
8
9
WESTERN ISLES
Rubha Robhanais (Butt of Lewis)
Eoropaidh
Port Nis
Lional
Tabost
Suainebost
Cros
Dail Bho Thuath
Dail Bho Dheas
Aird Dhail
Glen Cross
Cuidhaseadar
Toa Galson
Gabhsunn Bho Dheas
Gabhsunn Bho Thuath
A857
Mealabost
Coig Peighinnean
Siadar Uarach
Siadar Iarach
STEINACLEIT CAIRN & STANDING STONES
South Galson
Rubha Leathann
Baile an Truiseil
Barabhas
Bru
Arnol
Bragar
Labost
Fibhig
Siabost
Rinn Druim Tallig
Aird Mhor Bragair
Rubh'an Dunain
Dail Beag
Dail Mor
Mullach Charlabhaigh
Carlabhaigh
A858
Aird Mhor
Gearrannan
Craigeam
Borghastan
Loch Carlabhagh
CARLOWAY BROCH
Little Bernera
Tolastadh a Chaolais
Breascleit
Calanais
CALLANISH STANDING STONES
Loch Roag
West Loch Roag
Gallan Head
Aird Uig
Bhaltos
Tobson
Pabaidh Mor
Vacsay
Great Bernera
Breacleit
Bernera
Kirkibost
Tacleit
Cnip
Uigen
Timsgearraidh
Miabhig
Cradhlastadh
Eadar Dha Fhadhail
Cairisiadar
Crulabhig
Geisiadar
Linsiadar
Gearraidh na h-Aibhne
Griomarstaidh
Loch Tarbhairt
Ben Drovinish
Forsnaval 205
Aird Mhor Mangersta
Mangurstadh
Loch Sgailabhat
Suainaval 429
Aird Fenish
Aird Brenish
Islibhig
Breanais
Mealasta
Mealasta Island
Mealisval 574
Tahaval 515
Cracaval 514
Tamanaisval 467
Griomaval
Loch Suainaval
Loch Raonasgail
Eileanan Fenish
Loch Grunavat
Einacleit
Scealascro
Giosla
Loch Croistean
Loch Dibadale
Beinn Mheadhonach 397
Skeun 265
Coduinn 241
Maghannan
Loch Morsgail
Loch Langavat
Morsgail Forest
EILEAN LEODHAIS (LEWIS)
Teahaval 256
Loch Tungavat
Callanish Bheag 226
Callanish Mhor 228
Beinn Mohal 207
Loch Airigh na h-Airde
Loch Coirigerod
Roineval 281
Loch Strandavat
Loch Erisort
Sleiteachal Mhor 248
Kintarvie
Stornoway (Steornabhagh)
Stornoway Harbour
Newmarket
Laxdale
Sandwick
Melbost
Aignis
Garrabost
Sanndabhaigh
Tunga
Col
Col Sands
Aird Thunga
Broch
Bac
Gress
Griais
Loch a Tuath
Port Nan Giuran
Sron Ruadh
Rubha Bhataisgeir
Creag Fhraoch
Melbost Sands
Arnish Moor
Arnish Pt
Rubh a' Bhaigh Uaine
Grimsiadar
Crosbost
Liurbost
Leurbost
Raerinish Point
Tabhaigh Mhor
Orasaigh
Torraigh
Marthig
Calbost
Rubha Iosal
Gleann Ghrabhair
Cabharstadh
Gearraidh Bhaird
Cearsiadar
Tabost
Baile Ailein
Lacasaigh
Caos
Eilean Chaluim Chille
B8060
Airidh a' Bhruaich
Ceann Loch Shiphoirt
Glen Ouirn
Loch Shandabhat
Grabhair
Tom an Fhuadain
Kebock Head
Gob na Milaid
Leumrabhagh
Eisgean
Loch Shell
Eilean Iubhard
Srianach
Caolas Eilean Iubhard
Mulhagery
Uisenis 371
Crionaig 470
Corlabhadh
Tathas Mhor
Eilean Mor A'Bhaigh
Rubha Bhrollum
Rubh a'Bhaird
Sgeir na h-Eigheach
Gob Rubh'Uisenis
Mol Truisg
Park
Shiant Islands
Garbh Eilean 161
Eilean Mhuire
Eilean an Tighe
SOUND OF SHIANT
EILEAN HEARADH (HARRIS)
Seaforth Island
Loch Seaforth
Aird a' Mhulaidh
Athlinne
Maraig
Kenmore
Reinigeadal
Caiteshal 449
Toddun 528
Straiaval 389
Sgaoth Aird 559
Clett Ard
Mulla-fo-dheas 743
Clisham 799
Uisgnaval Mor 729
Stulaval 579
Mullach a' Ruisg 473
Liuthaid 492
Beinn a' Mhuil 370
Kearnaval 378
Rapaire 453
Beinn a'Bhoth 308
Scalaval Sandig
Loch Voshimid
Mas a'Chnoic-chuairtich 386
Mullach na Reidheachd 295
Uillaval 659
Oreval 662
Cleiseval 511
Tirga Mor 679
Forest of Harris
Husival Mor 489
Sgianait 425
Loch a'Ghlinne
Huisinis
Husinish Point
Scarp
Sron Romul 308
Kearstay
Mol Quinn
Liongam
Aird Bheag
Aird Mhor
Gob na h-Airde Moire
Loch Resort
Loch Bodavat
Caolas an Eilein
Loch Tamanavay
Horsanish
Rubha Bhrataic
Arda Beaga
Gobhaig
Abhainnsuidhe
Taransay Glorigs
Soay Beg
Soay Mor
Miabhag
Bun Abhainn Eadarra
Aird Asaig
West Loch Tarbert
Tarransaigh
Ben Raah 267
Aird Vanish
Paible
Rubha Sgeirigin
Sound of Taransay
Beinn Dhubh 506
Beesdale
Ceann Reamhar 467
Taobh Siar
Tairbeart (Tarbert)
Urgha
Losgaintir
Corran Seilebost
South Harris Forest 287
Seilebost
A859
Carragheh
Scalpaigh
Eilean Scalpaigh (Scalpay)
Kennavay
Meall Chaillbost
East Loch Tarbert
Meanhag
Rubha Romagi
Rubha Mas a'Chnuic
Toe Head
Chaipaval 365
Ciett Nisabost
Burgh
Bulabhall 354
Heileasbhal Mor 384
Sgarasta Mhor
Bleaval 398
Aird Mhige
Liceasto
Leac a'Li
Greosabhagh
Stockinish
Cluer
Rubha Bocaig
Rubha Cluer
SOUTH HARRIS
Traigh na Cleavag
Taobh Tuath
Maodal
Loch Langavat
Aird Leimhe
Manais
Fleoideabhagh
Ard Manish
Cuidhtinis
Loch Fleoideabhagh
Rubha Quidnish
Finsbay
Boirseam
Ceann A Bhaigh
Lingarabay Island
An t-Ob
Roneval 459
Strondeval 211
Cairminis
Stranndha
Roghadal
ST CLEMENT'S CHURCH
Rubha Vallarip
Renish Point
Ensay
Killegray
Shillay
Sound of Shillay
Pabbay
Beinn a'Charnain 196
Baileanacille
Quinish
SOUND of Pabbay
Eilean Bhearnaraigh (Berneray)
Borve Hill 85
Rusigearraidh
Borgh
Boreray
Massacamber
Sound of Berneray
Port Nan Long
Newton
Lingay
Groay
Gilsay
Scaravay
Aird Thormaid
SOUND OF HARRIS
Fladda-chuain
Gaeilavore
Gearran Island
Rubha Hunish
72
73

G
H
J
K
L
M
N
THE MINCH
Kinlochbervie
Oldshore More
Blairmore
Sheigra
Achlyness
Rhiconich
Fanagmore
Tarbet
Foindle
Handa Island
Laxford Bridge
Badnabay
Scourie
Badcall
Eddrachillis Bay
Kylestrome
Unapool
Drumbeg
Nedd
Newton
Point of Stoer
Culkein
Raffin
Achnacarnin
Clashnessie
Balchladich
Stoer
Clachtoll
Little Assynt
Rhicarn
Achmelvich
Ardroe
Baddidarach
Lochinver
Strathan
Badnaban
Inverkirkaig
Glencanisp Forest
Suilven
Canisp
Stronechrubie
Rubha Coigeach
Enard Bay
Rhegreanoch
Reiff
Altan Dubh
Polbain
Achiltibuie
Polglass
Isle Ristol
Summer Isles
Ardnagoine
Tanera Beg
Achvraie
Achduart
Culnacraig
Ledbeg
Elphin
Knockan
Drumrunie
Drumrunie Forest
Cul Mor
Cul Beag
Stac Polly
Strathkanaird
Priest Island
Bottle Island
Isle Martin
Ardmair
Rhue
Morefield
Ullapool
Braes of Ullapool
Rhidorroch
Rhidorroch Forest
Greenstone Point
Opinan
Mellon Udrigle
Gruinard Island
Gruinard Bay
Achgarve
Laide
Mellon Charles
Ormiscaig
Aultbea
Bualnaluib
Drumchork
First Coast
Second Coast
Little Gruinard
Mungasdale
Badluarachrach
Scoraig
Achmore
Rhireavach
Little Loch Broom
Dundonnell
Badrallach
Allt na h-Airbhe
Camusnagaul
Ardessie
Loch Broom
Blarnalevoch
Loggie
Rhiroy
Ardindrean
Letters
Leckmelm
Ardcharnich
Inverlael Forest
Inverbroom
Auchlunachan
Glackour
Auchindrean
Fasagrianach
Braemore
Strathnasheallag Forest
Fisherfield Forest
An Teallach
Rubha Reidh
Cove
Melvaig
Aultgrishan
Inverasdale
Midtown
Naast
Peterburn
North Erradale
Boor
Poolewe
Londubh
Tournaig
Inverewe
Loch Ewe
Isle of Ewe
Big Sand
Carn Dearg
Gairloch
Auchtercairn
Mial
Longa Island
A835
A832
A837
A894
A838
B869
80
74

A
B
C
D
E
F
G
1
2
3
4
5
6
7
8
9
Cape Wrath
Duslic
Kearvaig
Danger Zone
Inshore
Balnakeil
Durness
Keoldale
Leirinmore
Sangobeg
Rispond
Sarsgrum
Whiten Head
Rubha Thormaid
Midfield
Talmine
Skerray
Modsarie
Torrisdale
Bettyhill
Achina
Invernaver
Skullomie
Coldbackie
Tongue
Borgie
Borgie Forest
Farr
Kyle of Tongue
Ribigill
Midtown
Achuvoldrach
Hope
Heilam
Lochside
Portnacon
Laid
Eriboll
Polla
Loch Eriboll
Sheigra
Balchrick
Blairmore
Oldshore Beg
Oldshore More
Kinlochbervie
Badcall
Achriesgill
Rhiconich
Achlyness
Fanagmore
Tarbet
Foindle
Handa Island
Laxford Bridge
Badnabay
Scourie More
Scourie
Badcall
Eddrachillis Bay
Kylestrome
Unapool
Reay Forest
Achfary
Kinloch
Aultanrynie
Strath More
Alltnacaillich
Allnabad
Mudale
Altnaharra
Kilbreck
Loch Naver
Strathnaver
Syre
Skail
Crask Inn
Strath Vagastie
Loch Shin
Strath Tirry
Rhian
Shinness Lodge
Dalmichy
Achnairn
Colaboll
Lairg
Sallachy
Savalmore
Balchars
Tomich
Torroble
Rhaoine
Muie
Ardochu
Strath Fleet
Pittentrail
Achinduich
Invershin
Inveran
Linsidemore
Culrain
Kyle of Sutherland
Bonar Bridge
Ardgay
Kincardine
Ardchronie
Migdale
Spinningdale
Kyloag
Balblair
Tulloch
Drumbeg
Nedd
Clashnessie
Newton
Little Assynt
Loch Assynt
Inchnadamph
Stronechrubie
Ledmore
Elphin
Knockan
Lochinver
Inverkirkaig
Strathan
Baddidarach
Ardroe
Rhegreanoch
Drumrunie
Ardmair
Ullapool
Morefield
Rhue
Strathcanaird
Rhidorroch Forest
Oykel Bridge
Lubcroy
Langwell
Glen Oykel
Invercassley
Rosehall
Altass
Achnahanat
Auchinduich
Duchally
Glenmuick
Badintagairt
Overscaig Hotel
Corrykinloch
Glen Cassley
Braes of Ullapool
Leckmelm
Ardcharnich
Letters
Loggie
Strathcarron
The Craigs
Croick
Sgodachail
Amat Forest
Dounie
Soyal
A838
A836
A894
A837
A835
A839
A949
B869
B873
B871
B801
79
75

82
Island of Stroma
Langaton Point
Nethertown
Uppertown
Dunnet Head
Easter Head
Stromness
DUNCANSBY HEAD
John o' Groats
Huna
Canisbay
Gills
East Mey
Mey
Harrow
Scarfskerry
Ham
Rattar
Brough
Dunnet
Barrock
Inkstack
Upper Gills
Brabster
Everley
Freswick
Skirza
Skirza Head
Ness Head
Auckengill
Nybster
Keiss
Tang Head
Stain
Sinclair's Bay
Reiss
Ackergill
Wick
Staxigore
North Head
South Head
Wick Bay
Hempriggs House
Whiterow
Thrumster
Sarclet
Ulbster
Whaligoe
Bruan
East Clyth
Mid Clyth
Occumster
Blackness
Lybster
Swiney
Forse
Latheron
Latheronwheel
Dunbeath
Dunbeath Bay
Inver
Toremore
Ramscraigs
Borgue
Newport
Berriedale
Ousdale
Badbea
Ord of Caithness
Navidale
East Helmsdale
Helmsdale
West Helmsdale
Gartymore
Portgower
Crakaig
Kilmote
Lothbeg
Lothbeg Point
Lothmore
Kintradwell
Greenhill
Dalchalm
Brora
Doll
Clynelish
West Clyne
Achrimsdale
Carrol
Killin
Gordonbush
Kilbraur
Backies
Golspie
Dunrobin Castle
Kirkton
Culmaily
Aberscross
Littleferry
Loch Fleet
Skelbo
Fourpenny
Embo
Embo Street
Pitgrudy
Dornoch
Dornoch Point
Dornoch Sands
Tarbat Ness
Wilkhaven
Port Mor
Danger Zone
Thurso
Thurso Bay
Scrabster
Holborn Head
Crosskirk
Lybster
Bridge of Forss
Viewfield
Janetstown
Ormwe
Clardon
Murkle
Castletown
Haimer
Olrig House
Hayfield
Greenland
Thurdistoft
Tain
Lochside
Reaster
Bowermadden
Lyth
Sortat
Alterwall
Slickly
Lochend
Howe
Mireland
Kirk
Hastigrow
Halcro
Bowertower
Tister
Corsback
Lynegar
North Watten
Watten
Mains of Watten
Killimster
Winless
Sibster
Quoys of Reiss
Halkirk
Georgemas Junc. Sta.
Gerston
Calder Mains
Skinnet
Braal Castle
Spittal
Mybster
Harpsdale
Achies
Olgrinmore
Bloody Moss
Dorrery
Scotscalder Sta.
Brawlbin
Shurrery
Shurrery Lodge
Broubster
Forsie
Shebster
Achvarasdal
Buldoo
Reay
Sandside House
Dounreay
Fresgoe
Bighouse
Melvich
Portskerra
Strathy
Strathy Point
Baligill
Totegan
Brawl
Aultiphurst
Lednagullin
Golval
Kirkton
Achiemore
Craigtown
Dalhalvaig
Croick
Trantlemore
Trantlebeg
Forsinain
Forsinard
Strath Halladale
Altnabreac Sta.
Lochdhu Hotel
Dalganachan
Westerdale
Tormsdale
Tacher
Stemster
Achavanich
Sheppardstown
Upper Lybster
Reisgill
Nottingham
Houstry
Smerral
Badnagie
Knockally
Achnaclyth
Braemore
Achorn
Langwell House
Wag
Langwell
Aultibea
Kildonan Lodge
Kinbrace
Burnfoot
Achentoul
Badanloch Lodge
Altanduin
Duible
Torrish
Kilphedir
Caen
Marrel
Craggie
Gobernuisgeach
G H L A N D
A9
A99
A836
A882
A897
B871
B874
B876
B870
B855
A839
A949

A
B
C
D
E
F
G
H
J
1
2
3
4
5
6
7
8
9
10
11
12
ORKNEY
NORTH RONALDSAY
PAPA WESTRAY
WESTRAY
THE NORTH SOUND
SANDAY
EDAY
ROUSAY
STRONSAY
SHAPINSAY
Kirkwall
Stromness
HOY
FLOTTA
BURRAY
SOUTH RONALDSAY
SCAPA FLOW
PENTLAND FIRTH
Island of Stroma
DUNNET HEAD
DUNCANSBY HEAD
John o' Groats
Thurso
Castletown
HIGHLAND
Pentland Skerries
Copinsay
Auskerry
Egilsay
Wyre
Gairsay
Swona
Old Man of Hoy
Stronsay Firth
Sanday Sound
Westray Firth
Shapinsay Sound
Wide Firth
St Margaret's Hope
Dunnet
Mey
Canisbay
Auckengill
Keiss
Wick
Lybster

J
K
L
M
N
P
Q
R
S
1
2
3
4
5
6
7
8
9
10
11
12
SHETLAND
UNST
YELL
FETLAR
WHALSAY
BRESSAY
PAPA STOUR
MUCKLE ROE
ST MAGNUS BAY
Muckle Flugga
Herma Ness
The Noup
Haroldswick
Norwick
Baltasound
Uyeasound
Belmont
Gutcher
Cullivoe
Mid Yell
Burravoe
Ulsta
West Sandwick
Toft
Mossbank
Sullom Voe Oil Terminal
Brae
Voe
Hillswick
North Roe
Lunna Holm
Out Skerries
Vidlin
Symbister
Walls
Sandness
Aith
Bixter
Lerwick
Scalloway
Bressay
Fitful Head
Sumburgh Head
Sumburgh Roost
Bergen (Norway) (Summer Only)
Stromness and Aberdeen
10 miles
10 km

INDEX TO PLACE NAMES

Use of the index

The letters and numbers around the page edges of the main map section form the referencing system used in this atlas.

The place name is followed by a page number and a grid reference specific to that page. The place name can be found by searching that grid square. Where more than one place has the same name, each can be distinguished by the abbreviated county or council name shown after the place name.

Abbreviations

A list of counties (England) and unitary authorities (England, Scotland & Wales) is given with their abbreviated form used in this index.

Aber.	Aberdeenshire
Aber.C.	Aberdeen City
Arg. & B.	Argyll & Bute
B. & H.	Brighton & Hove
B. & N.E.Som.	Bath & North East Somerset
B.Gwent	Blaenau Gwent
Beds.	Bedfordshire
Berks.	Berkshire
Bourne.	Bournemouth
Bristol	City & County of Bristol
Bucks.	Buckinghamshire
Caerp.	Caerphilly
Cambs.	Cambridgeshire
Carmar.	Carmarthenshire
Cere.	Ceredigion
Chan.I.	Channel Islands
Ches.	Cheshire
Cornw.	Cornwall
Cumb.	Cumbria
D. & G.	Dumfries & Galloway
Darl.	Darlington Borough
Denb.	Denbighshire
Derby	Derby City
Derbys.	Derbyshire
Dundee	Dundee City
Dur.	County Durham
E.Ayr.	East Ayrshire
E.Dun.	East Dunbartonshire
E.Loth.	East Lothian
E.Renf.	East Renfrewshire
E.Riding	East Riding of Yorkshire
E.Suss.	East Sussex
Edin.	City of Edinburgh
Falk.	Falkirk
Flints.	Flintshire
Glas.	Glasgow City
Glos.	Gloucestershire
Gt.Lon.	Greater London
Gt.Man.	Greater Manchester
Gwyn.	Gwynedd
H. & W.	Hereford & Worcester
Hants.	Hampshire
Hart.	Hartlepool
Herts.	Hertfordshire
High.	Highland
I.o.A.	Isle of Anglesey
I.o.M.	Isle of Man
I.o.S.	Isles of Scilly
I.o.W.	Isle of Wight
Inclyde.	Inverclyde
Lancs.	Lancashire
Leic.C.	Leicester City
Leics.	Leicestershire
Lincs.	Lincolnshire
Luton	Luton Borough
M.K.	Milton Keynes
M.Tyd.	Merthyr Tydfil
Mersey.	Merseyside
Middbro.	Middlesbrough
Midloth.	Midlothian
Mon.	Monmouthshire
N.Ayr.	North Ayrshire
N.E.Lincs.	North East Lincolnshire
N.Lan.	North Lanarkshire
N.Lincs.	North Lincolnshire
N.P.T.	Neath Port Talbot
N.Som.	North Somerset
N.Yorks.	North Yorkshire
Nhumb.	Northumberland
Norf.	Norfolk
Northants.	Northamptonshire
Notts.	Nottinghamshire
Ork.	Orkney
Oxon.	Oxfordshire
P. & K.	Perth & Kinross
Pembs.	Pembrokeshire
Ports.	Portsmouth City
R. & C.	Redcar & Cleveland
R.C.T.	Rhondda Cynon Taff
Renf.	Renfrewshire
Rut.	Rutland County
S'ham	Southampton City
S.Ayr.	South Ayrshire
S.Glos.	South Gloucestershire
S.Lan.	South Lanarkshire
S.Yorks.	South Yorkshire
Sc.Bord.	Scottish Borders
Shet.	Shetland
Shrop.	Shropshire
Som.	Somerset
Staffs.	Staffordshire
Stir.	Stirling
Stock.	Stockton-on-Tees
Stoke.	City of Stoke-on-Trent
Suff.	Suffolk
Surr.	Surrey
Swan.	Swansea
Swin.	Swindon Borough
T. & W.	Tyne & Wear
V. of Glam.	Vale of Glamorgan
W.Dun.	West Dunbartonshire
W.Isles	Western Isles
W.Loth.	West Lothian
W.Mid.	West Midlands
W.Suss.	West Sussex
W.Yorks.	West Yorkshire
Warks.	Warwickshire
Wilts.	Wiltshire
Wrex.	Wrexham

Great Britain